Business Scenarios

A Context-Based Approach to Business Communication

D1444128

Business Scenarios

A Context-Based Approach to Business Communication

Heidi Schultz, Ph.D.
Kenan-Flagler Business School
The University of
North Carolina at
Chapel Hill

**McGraw-Hill
Irwin**

Boston   Burr Ridge, IL   Dubuque, IA   Madison, WI   New York
San Francisco   St. Louis   Bangkok   Bogotá   Caracas   Kuala Lumpur
Lisbon   London   Madrid   Mexico City   Milan   Montreal   New Delhi
Santiago   Seoul   Singapore   Sydney   Taipei   Toronto

The *McGraw·Hill* Companies

McGraw-Hill
Irwin

BUSINESS SCENARIOS:
A CONTEXT-BASED APPROACH TO BUSINESS COMMUNICATION
Published by McGraw-Hill/Irwin, a business unit of The McGraw-Hill Companies, Inc., 1221 Avenue of
the Americas, New York, NY, 10020. Copyright © 2006 by The McGraw-Hill Companies, Inc. All rights
reserved. No part of this publication may be reproduced or distributed in any form or by any means, or
stored in a database or retrieval system, without the prior written consent of The McGraw-Hill Companies,
Inc., including, but not limited to, in any network or other electronic storage or transmission, or broadcast
for distance learning.

Some ancillaries, including electronic and print components, may not be available to customers outside the
United States.

This book is printed on acid-free paper.

1 2 3 4 5 6 7 8 9 0 DOC/DOC 0 9 8 7 6 5 4

ISBN 0-07-298424-4

Editorial director: *John E. Biernat*
Publisher: *Andy Winston*
Sponsoring editor: *Barrett Koger*
Developmental editor: *Megan Gates*
Editorial assistant: *Peter Vanaria*
Marketing manager: *Keari Bedford*
Senior project manager: *Susanne Riedell*
Manager, New book production: *Heather D. Burbridge*
Senior designer: *Adam Rooke*
Senior media project manager: *Rose M. Range*
Developer, Media technology: *Brian Nacik*
Typeface: *10/12 Times Roman*
Compositor: *Interactive Composition Corporation*
Printer: *R. R. Donnelley*

Library of Congress Cataloging-in-Publication Data

Schultz, Heidi Maria.
    Business scenarios : a context-based approach to business communication / Heidi
Schultz. -- 1st ed.
        p. cm.
    Includes bibliographical references and index.
    ISBN 0-07-298424-4 (alk. paper)
    1. Business communication. 2. Business writing. 3. Oral communication.
4. Context (Linguistics) I. Title.
HF5718.S325 2006
651.7--dc22   2004060998

www.mhhe.com

Dedication

To
Helga, who loves "business and industry,"
and
Hans, who contributed to the visuals.

About the Author

Heidi Schultz is Professor and Director of Management and Corporate Communication at the Kenan-Flagler Business School, University of North Carolina at Chapel Hill. She teaches oral and written business communication at the undergraduate, MBA, executive MBA, and Executive Education levels. Her research emphasizes electronic communication issues as well as the presentation styles of successful business professionals. She is the author of the book *The Elements of Electronic Communication.*

Her corporate and executive clients include American Financial Services Association, Analytical Sciences, Inc., Cisco, GlaxoSmithKline, the Environmental Protection Agency, Misys Health Care, Performance Food Group, SunTechMed, Syngenta, the U.S. Postal Service, W.C. Bradley, Xerox, public health managers, and sports managers.

In 1997, she started UNC's Kenan-Flagler's Business Communication Center, which has grown to serve the communication needs of all business students. She also directed the Writing Center at UNC-Chapel Hill.

Heidi received her Ph.D. from UNC-Chapel Hill, M.A. from UNC-Charlotte, and B.A. from Lenoir-Rhyne College.

I have to be honest—I hate to write. It takes time and it's hard, and now I'm faced with having to write a preface. I'm kind of embarrassed too, because I know I sound a lot "whinier" than any of my own students ever have. Even so, I'm going to try to come up with something to make my editors happy. So here goes. . . .

As I see it, the preface is a kind of justification for a book. It says, "There's a need that this book seeks to fill." To that end, *Business Scenarios* addresses rhetorical issues within the context of authentic and complex business situations. These scenarios offer communication-related challenges you'll resolve through lively class discussion, debate, and . . . yes, through writing and speaking!

In short, *Business Scenarios* avoids a prescriptive approach to learning business communication; rather, it teaches you how to make informed rhetorical choices that you can adapt to the complexities of any business situation.

OK—I think I'll stop with that. Enjoy the book, and email me if you have questions or suggestions. Heidi_Schultz@unc.edu.

Acknowledgments

I want to thank the following people for helping make my ideas and writing better. They are

My wonderful students—past, present, and future

My sister: Helen

My most excellent, erudite, and entertaining colleagues: Judy Tisdale, Lynn Setzer, Patty Harms, Tim Flood, and Melody van Lidth de Jeude

My ever-patient editors at McGraw-Hill: Linda Schreiber, Megan Gates, and Barrett Koger

My insightful reviewers

Laura Barelman, *Wayne State University*

Paula E. Brown, *Northern Illinois University*

Dale Cyphert, *University of Northern Iowa*

Susan Fiechtner, *Texas A&M University*

Dina Friedman, *University of Massachusetts–Amherst*

Larry Honl, *University of Wisconsin–Eau Claire*

William King Thunderbird, *Garvin School of International Management*

William R. Kohler, *University of Illinois–Chicago*

Diana McKowen, *Indiana University*

Rolf Norgaard, *University of Colorado–Boulder*

Diane Ramos, *Duquesne University*

Annette Veech, *Washington University at St. Louis*

Jeanne Weiland Herrick, *Northwestern University*

And most of all

My Adam***

Brief Contents

Contents

Document Design: Applying audience-centered techniques that increase your audience's reading efficiency.

Chapter 4
Wake Partners—The "New Conservative Mutual Fund"   53

Tone: Written words affect how your audience "hears" you.

Chapter 5
It Has Come to My Attention . . .   61

Short Business Messages: Writing informative, bad news, and persuasive messages.

Chapter 6
Payroll's Paperless Payday   67

Chapter 7
Do Not Park Here . . . or Here . . . or Here   77

Crisis Communication.

Chapter 13
Let's Go Out to Eat   115

Chapter 14
District of Columbia Water and Sewer Authority—Communicating Health Hazards to the Public   129

CHAPTER 1

Business Writing Basics

Chapter Emphasis and Rationale

This section provides some of the key punctuation, grammar, and editing techniques you'll want to use in effective business writing. Keep in mind, however, this section doesn't cover ALL the grammar, punctuation, and mechanics rules in the universe. It just addresses a few key concepts that any successful businessperson needs to know. I'm not suggesting that the other rules don't matter. Far from that. I'm a stickler for the rules. However, I also know that business readers are different from us English-teacher types. Business readers want clarity and efficiency . . . on the first read![1]

Punctuation—A Brief History, Rationale,[2] and Key Points

Have you ever stopped to ask yourself, "What is punctuation"? Gosh, I hope not. But it's an interesting question, nonetheless. It's really kind of a cryptic system of dots and dashes . . . not unlike Morse code . . . used by writers to send signals to readers. Indeed, punctuation is "a courtesy designed to help readers understand a story without stumbling."[3]

What's interesting is that the earliest writing didn't have punctuation at all. So knowing, for example, when a complete thought ended and another started was often left to interpretation and resulted, no doubt, in lots of stumbling. As with spelling, punctuation became standardized after Johannes Gutenberg invented the printing press in Germany in the mid 15th century. That's because the printed word—through its printed permanence—preserves standards. What's also interesting, however, is that early punctuation was devised more for speakers than for readers. For example, commas told speakers where to pause for emphasis. Then around the 18th century, grammarians

---

[1] Jeanette Gilsdorf and Don Leonard have written an interesting article on how business executives respond to usage errors. As you might guess, "academics are more bothered about usage, on average, than executives are" (p. 459). See, "Big Stuff, Little Stuff: A Decennial Measurement of Executives' and Academics' Reactions to Questionable Usage Elements." *The Journal of Business Communication* 38, no. 4 (October 2001), pp. 439–75.

[2] http://www.nyu.edu/classes/copyXediting/Punctuation.html, accessed May 16, 2004.

[3] Lynn Truss. *Eats Shoots and Leaves: The Zero Tolerance Approach to Punctuation* (New York: Gotham Books, 2003), p. 7.

developed a system of punctuation based on structure rather than on sound. You can thank—or blame—them.

So while it can be annoying when your writing teacher holds you accountable for something as seemingly trivial as punctuation, you need to master some punctuation so your readers get your meaning the first time through. That's particularly important for today's time-strapped businesspeople.

Punctuate with Pizzazz

, Commas—When to Use the Pesky Critters

I keep singing the 1980s Boy George song over and over in my head:

> *Karma Karma Karma Karma*
> *Karma Chameleon*
> *You come and go*
> *You come and go*

Except my version goes like this:

> *Comma, Comma, Comma, Comma*
> *Coma Chameleon*
> *Where do you go?*
> *Where do you go?*

Pattern 1   What's a SOBFAN? It's someone who sobs when his favorite sports team loses. I was a SOBFAN during the UNC Tarheel's 2002–2003 basketball season. SOBFAN is also a convenient way to remember the "coordinating conjunctions." Take a look:

S = so

O = or

B = but

F = for

A = and

N = nor

Now if I continue to sob and make a . . . well, you know the word, . . . it's a synonym for derriere . . . anyway, if I continue to sob and make a derriere out of myself, then I'm a SOBFANY.

Y = yet

So here's how you use these words—known in polite circles as "coordinating conjunctions." If you have *two complete sentences* and join those sentences with one of the SOBFANYs, then you need a comma *before* that SOBFANY.

Here's the pattern:

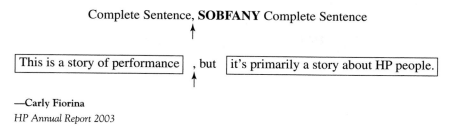

Complete Sentence, **SOBFANY** Complete Sentence

This is a story of performance , but it's primarily a story about HP people.

—**Carly Fiorina**
HP Annual Report 2003

Pattern 2   If you start with an incomplete sentence—something like an introductory phrase—you need to follow it with a comma.
Here's the pattern:

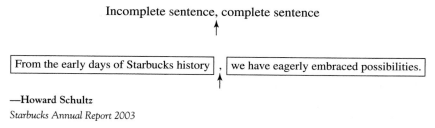

Incomplete sentence, complete sentence

From the early days of Starbucks history , we have eagerly embraced possibilities.

—**Howard Schultz**
Starbucks Annual Report 2003

If the introductory phrase is short, it's OK to leave out the comma. Remember, your goal is to minimize "misreading."

Pattern 3   If you want to insert an idea between a complete sentence, you'll need commas to separate the inserted idea.
Here's the pattern:

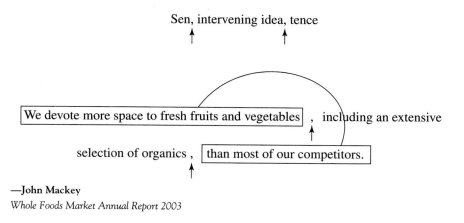

Sen, intervening idea, tence

We devote more space to fresh fruits and vegetables , including an extensive

selection of organics , than most of our competitors.

—**John Mackey**
Whole Foods Market Annual Report 2003

Pattern 4   I need to tell you about one more pattern, and then I'll leave you alone.

When you want to include a list of *three or more* words or phrases, you need to separate them with a comma. Make a note of the last comma.

Here's the pattern:

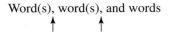

Word(s), word(s), and words

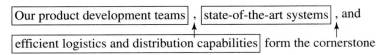

Our product development teams , state-of-the-art systems , and efficient logistics and distribution capabilities form the cornerstone from which we can continue to build and deliver excellent product[s] with great value.

—**Pete Bonepath**
Jones Apparel Annual Report 2003

Sometimes writers will leave off the last comma, as in the following example.

Canada (both English- and French-speaking provinces), Australia, the United Kingdom and Mexico have embraced Krispy Kreme . . .

—**Scott A. Livengood**
Krispy Kreme Annual Report 2004

; Semicolons

This rule is SO easy. Semicolons and periods are interchangeable. Using one or the other is a matter of style. If you think two sentences "go together" for some rhetorical reason, then use a semicolon. Otherwise, use the old standby . . . the period.

Everywhere you look the signs are positive. Take a look at the charts accompanying this letter.

—**Anne M. Culcahy**
Xerox Annual Report 2003 (original)

Everywhere you look the signs are positive; take a look at the charts accompanying this letter.

—**Anne M. Culcahy**
Xerox Annual Report 2003 (with semicolon)

Dashes

These little lines are pretty powerful. They say to the reader, "Hey, stop, look what comes after me. Pay attention." So here are two easy rules:

Rule 1   The information that precedes the dash needs to be a complete sentence. The information that comes after can be anything—another sentence, a phrase, a series, or a word.

> Many of these initiatives increasingly reflect the integration of cross-functional disciplines, allowing us to leverage our resources, improve our efficiency, and increase our overall agility and speed—critical factors in sustaining our competitive advantage in a dynamic retail environment with a competitor as formidable as Wal-Mart.
>
> —**Bob Ulrich**
> *Target Annual Report 2003*

Rule 2   The sentence needs to start on one side of the dash and finish on the other side.

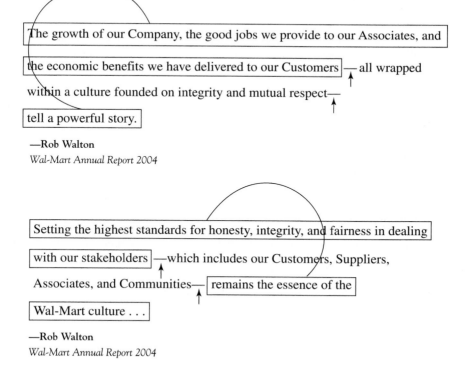

> The growth of our Company, the good jobs we provide to our Associates, and the economic benefits we have delivered to our Customers—all wrapped within a culture founded on integrity and mutual respect—tell a powerful story.
>
> —**Rob Walton**
> *Wal-Mart Annual Report 2004*

> Setting the highest standards for honesty, integrity, and fairness in dealing with our stakeholders—which includes our Customers, Suppliers, Associates, and Communities—remains the essence of the Wal-Mart culture . . .
>
> —**Rob Walton**
> *Wal-Mart Annual Report 2004*

Colons—Use Them When You Want to Emphasize What Comes After

Forgive me, but the theme to "Rawhide" keeps going through my head:

Rollin' rollin' rollin'
Though the streams are swollen,
Keep them doggies rolling,
Rawhide

. . . but just with different words . . .

The rollin' swollen colon
Like two dots goin' bowlin'
A clipped-off semi-colon,
Rawhide!

Pattern 1   The colon works this way in a *traditional* paragraph. The information that comes before that colon needs to be a complete sentence. The information that comes after can be just about anything else: another sentence, a phrase, a series, or a word. In the following example, the executives from Bed Bath and Beyond are talking about simplifying annual reports and financial statements:

> We stated our reasons for doing so last year, but the point is worth repeating here: we have simplified these documents because we believe your money is better spent where it matters most—in the stores, online, and in support of all we do as merchants.
>
> —Warren Eisenberg, Leonard Feinstein, Steven H. Termares
> *Bed Bath and Beyond Annual Report 2002*

Here's another example:

> We've learned some valuable lessons at Cadillac: In short, develop distinctly designed, high quality vehicles that truly delight the customer, create an ownership experience that reflects and reinforces the brand's image, support this with strong and innovative advertising, and the buyers will come.
>
> —Rick Wagner
> *GM Annual Report 2003*

Pattern 2   Now, lots of business documents include bulleted lists preceded by a colon. Here's the scoop. Either the information in front of the colon needs to be a complete sentence OR the bullets that follow the colon need to complete the thought.

Look at this schematic:

Pattern 2a   Sentence:

- Word, phrase, sentence, short paragraph
- Word, phrase, sentence, short paragraph
- Word, phrase, sentence, short paragraph

Pattern 2b   Fragment:

- Completed here with either a word or phrase
- Completed here with either a word or phrase
- Completed here with either a word or phrase

Here's an example of pattern 2a. The "set-up" information is a complete sentence.

This combination with Neuberger is ideal for several reasons:

- It dramatically increases the sale of our Client Services segment;
- It strengthens our presence in private wealth and asset management, particularly among high-net-worth investors;
- It should increase the consistency of our earnings and provide more opportunities for profitable growth;
- It provides us with a broader array of products and services for our clients; and
- Importantly, the partnership culture at Neuberger is a natural fit with Lehman Brothers' One Firm culture.

—**Richard S. Fuld, Jr.**
Lehman Brothers Annual Report 2003

Here's an example of pattern 2b. The "set-up" information gets completed in the bullets.

Other significant achievements included:

- Continuing successes in exploration, with major new discoveries in the deepwater U.S. Gulf of Mexico and Nigeria;
- Replacing more than 100 percent of production for the 11th consecutive year;
- Achieving significant progress in major upstream projects in Angola, Canada, Chad, Kazakhstan, Nigeria and Venezuela;
- Establishing a global natural gas business and achieving milestones in the commercialization of our vast Australian and West African gas resources;
- Significantly improving performance in refining and marketing.

—**Dave O'Reilly**
ChevronTexaco Annual Report 2003

Sentence Seeds and Patterns

To give your writing clarity and sophistication, you really just need to know about three things when constructing sentences: seeds, patterns, and lengths. So let's take a look at each.

Seeds

Where you plant your sentence seeds—your subject and your verb—can determine how clear your sentences are. Look at this example:

> The *combination* of effective monetary policy (embodied in the Federal Reserve's actions) along with a dynamic economy that *has produced* terrific gains in productivity has yielded great stability among prices.
> —Bradley C. Tank
> *The Strong Funds Annual Report 2001*

Here's one more example:

> Someone either internal or external to the organization is targeting an employee and in doing so is causing this employee to receive approximately 40 spam messages at a time. *We,* because of abuse with respect to our email system, because of the need to protect the privacy of our email communication, because of our need to cultivate an efficient workplace, and because we may be liable for inappropriate email messages subjected to you, *have asked* for a criminal investigation.

Understanding these sentences takes a lot of mental energy, and here's why: In the first example, 23 words separate the subject "combination" from the verb "has yielded," and in the second sentence, a whopping 43 words separate the subject "we" from the verb "have asked." While we could talk about ways to revise these sentences to limit the amount of cognitive overload they put on a poor reader's brain, I'd rather leave you with this guideline:

> Limit the number of words between your subjects and your verbs.

You'll be OK if you decide to insert a few words between subject and verb. Use your judgment about what constitutes "a few words."

Patterns

One of the challenges to writing clearly is showing the relationship between sentences. Here's the problem—a lot of basic writers fall into the subject-verb sentence pattern trap. Consider the following example:

> I drove to the store. The clerk sold me a printer cartridge. I went home. I installed it.

Is one idea the result of another? Does one idea cause another? Your readers aren't deliberately looking for the answers to these questions. It's not their job to make these kinds of logical connections—you have to do it for them. If you don't, your readers will move on to someone else's proposal, request, or idea.

If you take another look at these sentences, you'll notice each starts with a subject followed immediately by a verb:

I drove to the store. The **clerk sold** me a printer cartridge. **I went** home. **I installed** it.

By combining the sentences, you can show the logic.

I drove to the store where the clerk sold me a printer cartridge. As soon as I returned home, I installed it.

With this version, your readers know why you drove to the store and when you installed the cartridge. Moreover, the pattern isn't choppy or monotonous.

So now let's take a closer look at sentence patterns. Don't get too worried—we only need to look at three patterns! These patterns come from "complete" and "incomplete" sentences and follow one of the following patterns:

Pattern 1. Complete Incomplete

Pattern 2. Incomplete, Complete

Pattern 3. Com, Incomplete, Plete[4]

Here's a model sentence to show you how this concept works:

Matilda received a promotion. She got the promotion after just 3 months.

Pattern 1. Matilda received a promotion after just 3 months.

        [You don't need a comma in this pattern.]

Pattern 2. After just three months, Matilda received a promotion.[5]

        [You need a comma after the introductory phrase.]

Pattern 3. Matilda, after just 3 months, received a promotion.[6]

        [Notice that the sentence gets completed after the second comma.]

So when you write a business document, you'll want to go back through it and underline the subjects and verbs. If you have a series of sentences that follow the predictable, monotonous, and boring "subject verb" pattern, you'll need to show the relationship between those sentences. Combining those sentences in one of the three patterns is one way to show that relationship.

---

[4] The commas in each of the patterns are deliberate—so make a note of where they occur.

[5] This particular sentence also follows the rule for Comma Pattern 2.

[6] In this sentence, if you want to emphasize the information in between the commas, you may substitute the commas with dashes. If you want to de-emphasize the information in between the commas, you may substitute the commas with parentheses.

Let's look at one more example:

> The primary **means** of Super Bowl ticket distribution **is** through each NFL team. The general **public can't purchase** tickets any other way. The **NFL does not sell** tickets to ticket agents.

Here's a possible revision:

> The only way you can purchase Super Bowl tickets is through each NFL team. Because the NFL doesn't sell tickets to ticket agents, you can't buy tickets this way.

As you apply this technique to your writing, be sure your meaning is clear and you use as few words as possible.

Length

Strive for an average of 20 words per sentence. It's a good match for the short-term memory of busy readers.

Paragraph Patterns

I know you've heard about topic sentences before. They're supposed to introduce the theme or focus of each paragraph. And that's pretty good advice. Business readers need all the help they can get to understand your writing. But let me take another approach to talking about paragraph development by introducing you to a couple of paragraph patterns. They are the "explanation/description" pattern and the "list/number" pattern.

Explanation/Description Paragraphs

Explanation/description paragraphs are the standard model in reports and proposals. That's because this kind of paragraph clarifies and explains the key idea in the paragraph. Here's the pattern:

- Topic sentence
- Key ideas and/or unfamiliar ideas explained or expanded (if necessary)
- Example(s) of key ideas
- Answer to the "so what" question. "So what" if the paragraph is true? What's your conclusion? NOTE: Sometimes your "so what"—which could also be your rationale—comes earlier in the paragraph. And sometimes your "so what" might seem more logical at the end of an entire section.

Here's an example:

> Anheuser-Busch looks upon corporate citizenship as a serious and important responsibility. We have a long tradition of serving the communities in which we do business. In 2002, we provided disaster relief in the form of 55,000 cases of drinking water for distressed areas throughout the United States, increasing our

total water donations since 1988 to 1.7 million cases. Anheuser-Busch and its charitable foundation donated nearly $39 million to community organizations involved in education, health care, the arts, and conservation. . . . We believe that it's good business to invest in social norms and other forms of corporate citizenship. By providing meaningful solutions to promoting responsibility and curbing abuse, we are helping society.

—Patrick Stokes and August A. Busch

Anheuser-Busch 2002 Annual Report

> **Topic sentence:** Anheuser-Busch looks upon corporate citizenship as a serious and important responsibility.
>
> **Key idea of "corporate citizenship" expanded:** We have a long tradition of serving the communities in which we do business.
>
> **Example:** In 2002, we provided disaster relief in the form of 55,000 cases of drinking water for distressed areas throughout the United States, increasing our total water donations since 1988 to 1.7 million cases. Anheuser-Busch and its charitable foundation donated nearly $39 million to community organizations involved in education, health care, the arts, and conservation. . . .
>
> **So what?** We believe that it's good business to invest in social norms and other forms of corporate citizenship. By providing meaningful solutions to promoting responsibility and curbing abuse, we are helping society.

Let's look at another explanation/description paragraph with a slight twist:

To sustain the prominence of Starbucks brand in the marketplace and build stakeholder trust, we must be accountable for our actions. As a measure of our accountability, last year we published Starbucks first Corporate Social Responsibility Annual Report to provide transparency on our business practices, measurements of our performance, and benchmarks for future reporting. This year, we've taken additional steps to assure our stakeholders that the information in this report is accurate by engaging an independent third party to verify its contents.

—Howard Schultz and Orin C. Smith

Starbucks 2002 Annual Report

> **Topic sentence:** To sustain the prominence of Starbucks brand in the marketplace and build stakeholder trust, *we must be accountable for our actions.* ← **So what?**
>
> **Example:** As a measure of our accountability, last year we published Starbucks first Corporate Social Responsibility Annual Report to provide transparency on our business practices, measurements of our performance, and benchmarks for future reporting.
>
> **Example:** This year, we've taken additional steps to assure our stakeholders that the information in this report is accurate by engaging an independent third party to verify its contents.

List/Number Paragraphs

List/number paragraphs give you the opportunity to list items within a paragraph. Here's the pattern:

- Topic sentence
- Key ideas and/or unfamiliar ideas explained or expanded (if necessary)
- First . . . , Second . . . , Etc., . . . Finally
- Answer to the "so what" question. "So what" if the paragraph is true? What's your conclusion? NOTE: Sometimes your "so what"—which could also be your rationale—comes earlier in the paragraph. And sometimes your "so what" might seem more logical at the end of an entire section.

The following paragraph—which focuses on pension and postretirement health benefits—lists a series of itemized recommendations.

> Sears has undertaken a comprehensive evaluation of its domestic pension and post-retirement medical benefit plans to ensure that the benefits provided by the plans are the most appropriate for today's workforce and competitive landscape. Three important changes related to the company's pension and post-retirement medical benefit plans are being implemented as a result of this evaluation. First, Sears contributed $1.1 billion on a pretax basis to its domestic pension plan in 2003, placing the plan in a sounder financial and economic position, using proceeds from the sale of the Credit and Financial Products business and operating cash flows. Second, the company decided to enhance its 401(k) defined contribution plan and begin phasing out participation in its domestic pension plan. [Details omitted here] The third change in connection with the company's evaluation of its pension and post-retirement medical benefit plans involved a change in its accounting principle. [Details omitted here]
> —News release, January 29, 2004
> *Sears 4th Quarter 2003 results*

> Sears has undertaken a comprehensive evaluation of its domestic pension and post-retirement medical benefit plans *to ensure that the benefits provided by the plans are the most appropriate for today's workforce and competitive landscape.* ← **So what?**

> **Topic sentence announces the nature of the list:** Three important changes related to the company's pension and post-retirement medical benefit plans are being implemented as a result of this evaluation.

> **First point:** First, Sears contributed $1.1 billion on a pretax basis to its domestic pension plan in 2003, placing the plan in a sounder financial and economic position, using proceeds from the sale of the Credit and Financial Products business and operating cash flows.

Second point: Second, the company decided to enhance its 401(k) defined contribution plan and begin phasing out participation in its domestic pension plan. [Details omitted here]

Third and final point: The third change in connection with the company's evaluation of its pension and post-retirement medical benefit plans involved a change in its accounting principle. [Details omitted here]

Let me make a couple additional points about these templates. First, use these templates as starting points—then tweak them for your specific needs. Keep in mind that these patterns have some room for flexibility. Second, not all business paragraphs will fall into these patterns. That's OK. Just keep these patterns in your "arsenal of rhetorical tools" in case you get a brain freeze.

A final word about paragraph patterns: If you're writing a sequential paragraph—one that moves chronologically—be sure it moves from either

- Past to the present or
- Present to the future

This kind of organization implies progress, and that's a good thing in business. Here's a quick example:

> Innovation, a long-standing strategy at Anheuser-Busch, represents the path to greatness. Adolphus Busch employed this strategy more than **125 years ago** to make Budweiser the first national beer—using new ideas like pasteurizing beer, refrigerating railcars to transport it across the country and mobilizing grassroots salespeople to market the product. **Today,** Anheuser-Busch has some of the most innovative brewing, packaging and adventure-park facilities in the world.

Editing for Clear and Efficient Business Prose

I've heard people say "Good writing is good writing." But that view is simplistic. Rather, *context* has a lot to do with the characteristics of "good writing." Think for a moment about academic writing. First, you have a captive audience. Your professor *has* to read what you write. That's not the case in business. Businesspeople suffer from "information overload" and seek to streamline the massive amounts of information they have to process. They'll typically "give up" on your message if it isn't written in a way that's "audience-centered" in terms of "message digestibility" and document design. So "good writing" in an academic context may not be "good writing" in a business context.

Second, in academic writing, your professor prescribes a length. If you have to stretch an argument so it fulfills the page or word requirements, you'll pad phrases and repeat ideas. In business writing, you decide how long a document needs to be. If you pad phrases or repeat ideas, you will annoy your readers by wasting their time.

Third, academic writing seeks to mirror some aspect of your professor's expertise. For example, if your professor is an authority on the semiotics in Brazilian poetry and asks you to write a paper deconstructing a relevant poem, you're writing to an expert. In business, *you're* the expert. You're writing because you have expertise, information, and insights that others don't.

Fourth and finally, in academic writing, reality typically exists outside of most writers. As a result, academic writing embodies a more formal tone that avoids personal pronouns and contractions and accepts more passive voice constructions. In business writing, however, personal pronouns, contractions, and active voice create a conversational tone that business readers find more accessible.

Given these differences, business writing needs to be efficient. With this goal in mind, this section covers the following rhetorical concepts: camouflaged verbs, false starts, passive voice, plain English, contractions, personal pronouns, and redundancies.

Concealed, Cloaked, and Camouflaged Verbs

Camouflaged verbs—as the schematic below shows—are really nouns that hide verbs.

Verb + (-ation, -ant, -ency, -ent, -ion, -ment, -tion) = Verb in Camouflage (aka a Noun)

Look at this example:

We have made the decis**ion** to hire two new colleagues. (10 words)

Look at this possible revision now that I've extracted the verb from the noun:

We **decided** to hire two new colleagues. (7 words)

Here's another example. Notice the weak verb that accompanies this sentence:

Their current expansion strategy **is** a combina**tion** of acquisitions and alliances. (11 words)

Here's a possible revision:

Their current expansion strategy **combines** acquisition and alliances. (8 words)

If your word processing software allows, run your document through the "find" function and search for the endings that turn perfectly good, strong verbs into nouns.

Fake, Phony, Fictitious, False Subjects

These rhetorical constructions are "false" because they're abstractions. That is, they don't refer to any specific noun within the sentence or within previous sentences. They follow this formula:

It + a form of the verb "to be"

and

There + a form of the verb "to be"

"To be" and its equivalents
• Is
• Are
• Am
• Was
• Were
• Be
• Been
• Being
• Seems
• Appears
• And any variation

I have a few words of caution. **First,** not all "it is" constructions are false. When the "it" refers to a previous noun, "it" is acting as a pronoun with an antecedent.[7] For example:

> We must always do the right things in the right way, but we can also be more aggressive about telling our story. **It** is, after all, a great story . . .

—Lee Scott
Wal-Mart 2004 Annual Report

In this example, the "it is" is not a false subject because the "it" refers to "story." The "it" is the pronoun for the antecedent "story." Only when an "it" or a "there" doesn't refer to anything specific do we label it "false."

---

[7]*Antecedent* is the technical term for a noun to which the pronoun refers.

Let's look at one more example of a non–false subject:

My bologna has a first name,
__It's__ O-S-C-A-R
My bologna has a second name,
__It's__ M-A-Y-E-R. . . .
Oh, I love to eat it every day
And if you ask my why I'd say . . .
'Cause Oscar Mayer has a way with
B-O-L-O-G-N-A

Here again, "it's" is NOT a false subject because "it's" refers to bologna. Doesn't that make you want lunch?

One more example:

"Please read this **policy** carefully. **It** gives you important information about how we handle our personal information."

Second, these "false subjects" can occur anywhere in a sentence—not just at the start in the subject slot, as the following examples show:

> Recent preliminary data reviewed as part of the company's early warning system suggests [sic] that **there could be** an issue concerning the performance of these tires.
> —*http://www.firestone.com/news/news_index.asp?id+stx/040226b_rel*
> *Accessed May 22, 2004*

This revision contains four fewer words:

> Recent preliminary data reviewed as part of the company's early warning system suggest the performance of these tires could be an issue.

This particular example addresses the state of Alaska's Prince William Sound 15 years after the tanker *Exxon Valdez* ran aground there:

> Certainly **there were** severe short-term impacts on many species due to the spilled oil, and they suffered damages. But based on the studies of many scientists who have worked extensively in Prince William Sound, **there has been** no long-term damage caused by the spilled oil.
> —*http://www2.exxonmobil.com/corporate/Newsroom/NewsReleases/Corp_NR_Condition.asp*
> *Accessed May 26, 2004*

Here is a revision that reduces the original word count from 45 to 42:

> Certainly the spilled oil created severe short-term impacts on many species, and they suffered damages. But based on the studies of many scientists who have worked extensively in Prince William Sound, these species suffered no long-term damage caused by the spilled oil.

Let's look at another example from the same press release:

> **It is** ExxonMobil's position—and that of many independent scientists—that **there are** now no species in PWS [Prince William Sound] in trouble due to the impact of the 1989 oil spill.

This revision takes the original sentence from 32 to 24 words:

> ExxonMobil—and many independent scientists—agree that no species in PWS is currently in trouble due to the impact of the 1989 oil spill.

Third, sometimes "false subjects" sound more conversational or are just a part of our day-to-day conversational conventions as in the following example:

> It's raining.

In this case, the false subject is appropriate. How ridiculous we'd sound if—in trying to avoid the false subject here—we'd say or write:

> The clouds put forth rain.

Give me a break!

When you have a good reason for using false subjects, use them. Just be sure you're making an informed rhetorical choice to do so. Too many writers use "false subjects" randomly and indiscriminately. When they do, their writing is longer than it needs to be.

Here's an example:

> "At a time when many children lack significant role models and mentors, **it is** encouraging to see a company like Oscar Mayer step forward to help make a difference in the community and to those in need," said Judy Vredenburg, President and CEO of Big Brothers Big Sisters.
> —**Newsroom Press Release, New York, May 11, 2004**
> _www.kraft.com/newsroom_
> _Accessed May 21, 2004_

Vredenburg is speaking, so her false subject is natural. However, look at the revision anyway:

> "At a time when many children lack significant role models and mentors, I'm encouraged to see a company like Oscar Mayer step forward to help make a difference in the community and to those in need."

In the revision, we've reduced the number of words from 37 to 36. OK—so that change isn't earth-shattering. However, multiplied over the course of a document, these reductions do add up.

The following sentence—on the benefits of chewing gum—comes from the Wrigley's Gum Web site (www.wrigley.com):

> After meals, **it isn't** always convenient to use a toothbrush. (10 words)

> Chewing gum stimulates the production of saliva, which helps neutralize acids from foods that may cause tooth decay.

Here's a possible revision:

> After meals, brushing isn't always convenient. (6 words)

Finally, the "vague it" is a distant cousin to the "false subject." It (the "vague it" . . . just to be not vague) just takes up room without doing any work.

> Many outstanding companies found **it** impossible to meet their financial targets
> last year.
> —Dennis Koslowski
> *Tyco 2000 Annual Report*
> *http://www.tyco.com/pdf/2001AR/2001annual14_21.pdf*
> *Accessed May 26, 2004*

Here's the revision with "it" kicked out:

> Many outstanding companies could not meet their financial targets last year.

To keep your prose as lean as possible, get rid of the vague "it." And as we learned from recent corporate scandals, to keep your company as cLEAN as possible, get rid of the corrupt CEO.

Passive Voice

Look at these synonyms for "passive": inactive and submissive. These descriptions are the antithesis of good business practices. Good business practices should be active and assertive. And good business writing should reflect those practices.

Let's take a look at the problems passive voice causes.

Problem 1: Passive Voice Has a Pompous Tone

> The trademarks, logos, buttons and graphics contained in this Website **are owned**
> by DPSU or licensed to DPSU, and may not **be copied,** distributed, displayed,
> reproduced or transmitted, by any means, including electronic, mechanical,
> photocopying, recording, or otherwise, without the prior written permission of
> DPSU, except for personal or internal use. Use of third parties' likenesses, names
> and/or properties **is prohibited** without express written permission from such
> third parties.
> —Privacy Policy,[8] Dr. Pepper/Seven Up, Inc.
> *http://www.dpsu.com/privacy.html*
> *Accessed May 22, 2004*

---

[8]Privacy policies don't have to sound pompous. Consider the following excerpt from Campbell Soup's privacy policy: "Like most companies, we use 'cookie' technology on our sites to collect aggregate information. When you log into one of our sites, the cookie tells us whether you've visited us before or are a new visitor. This allows us to measure the appeal of our sites to new and return visitors. The cookie doesn't track any personal information about you or provide us with any way to contact you, and the cookie doesn't extract any information from your computer. Cookies are simply the best way for us to be able to offer you the most enjoyable and hassle-free online environment."
http://www.campbellsoupcompany.com/privacy_policy.asp, accessed May 22, 2004.

Problem 2: Passive Voice Can Make Your Sentences Longer, as the Following Example Shows

> The trademarks, logos, buttons and graphics contained in this Website **are owned** by DPSU . . . (14 words)

> DPSU owns the trademarks, logos, buttons and graphics contained in this Website . . . (12 words)

Here's another example:

> Each account **is managed** by a team of managers. (9 words)

> A team of managers manages each account. (7 words)

Problem 3: Passive Voice Leaves Out Information, Which a Reader Sometimes Needs or Wants This sentence comes from a news release Campbell's posted on its Web site in 2002 recalling cans labeled as "Campbell's Condensed Cream of Mushroom Soup" because those cans actually contained "Campbell's Chunky New England Clam Chowder":

> Consumers **are urged [by Campbell's? Health officials? Someone else?]** to return the product to the store where it **was purchased [by the consumer? By you? By someone else?]** for a full refund.

Here's the active voice:

> We'd like to urge you to return the product to the store where you bought it for a full refund.

Look at this sentence:

> Kool-aid Man, continually ranked by kids as one of the most-loved brand mascots, has **been honored [BY WHOM??? I want to know!]** with a footprint ceremony at Mann's Chinese Theatre in Hollywood. [Gosh, I wonder what Kool-aid Man's footprint looks like.]
> —*http://www.kraft.com/100/innovations/koolaidman.html*
> *Accessed May 22, 2004*

Here's another one:

> Although gas rationing kept the Wienermobile out of commission during World War II, it **was** later **received [BY WHOM??? Who received the Wienermobile?]** with overwhelming success when it toured to celebrate its 20th birthday in 1956.
> —*http://www.kraft.com/100/innovations/wienermobile.html*
> *Accessed May 22, 2004*

One more example:

> In the wake of events surrounding Martha Stewart's personal legal matters, MSO [Martha Stewart Omnimedia] has **been called** upon [BY WHOM???] to manage through unique and complex challenges.
> —**Sharon L. Patrick**
> *2003 Annual Report, http://ccbn.mobular.net/ccbn/7/635/684/*

When Do Writers Choose to Use Passive Voice?

Passive voice contributes to a pompous tone, can make sentences longer, and can leave out information a reader wants or needs. However, some clever writers will deliberately choose passive voice for several reasons:

1. When the writer wants to divorce the subject from the action. I call this rhetorical approach "deliberate strategic ambiguity."
2. When the writer wants to emphasize the receiver of rather than the doer of the action.
3. When the writer doesn't know the subject.
4. When all readers know the subject.

Let's look at each of these situations.

Reason 1 for Passive Voice: Deliberate Strategic Ambiguity   If you made a mistake, if revenues are down, or if your CEO unloaded lots of shares based on insider knowledge, then passive voice can come to your rescue. For example, in October 2002, Campbell's Soup inadvertently labeled its cans of "New England Clam Chowder" with "Cream of Mushroom" soup labels. This mislabeling happened because of a mistake at the plant's label controls. In response, Campbell's issued a warning targeted to people with shellfish allergies. Here's an excerpt from the press release:

> "Consumers **are urged** to return the product to the store where it **was purchased** for a full refund. . . . The recalled soup **was distributed** to 13 states through retail stores. . . . No illnesses have **been reported** to date."
> —**Press Release, October 4, 2002**
> *http://www.shareholder.com/campbell/ReleaseDetail.cfm?ReleaseID=91947*
> *Accessed May 22, 2004*

If I revise this excerpt to get rid of the passive constructions, here's what we'll get:

> Campbell's urges you to return the product to the store where you purchased it for a full refund. We recalled the soup, which we distributed to 13 states through retail stores. . . . No one has reported any illnesses to date.

Certainly, Campbell's is more explicitly responsible in the revision; the company is more implicitly responsible in the original. Keep in mind, however, I'm NOT suggesting passive is wrong. It just conveys a different tone.

In this example, Firestone has agreed to replace potentially defective tires:

> "The tires **were manufactured** in Joliette, Quebec, beginning in March 1999 through December 2002."
> —*http://www.firestone.com/news/news_index.asp?id+stx/040226b_rel*
> *Accessed May 22, 2004*

I find this sentence construction interesting because the press release doesn't say, "**Firestone** manufactured these [potentially dangerous and defective] tires," or "**We** manufactured these [potentially dangerous and defective] tires." Active voice takes responsibility while passive voice deflects responsibility.

In making a hiring, operations, or marketing blunder, I could say, "I made a mistake." However, saying "Mistakes were made" distances me from those mistakes.

Reason 2 for Passive Voice: Emphasis on Receiver Rather Than Doer of the Action
Sometimes the entity doing the action is less important than the entity receiving the action. Look at this "history" of "Shake 'n Bake":

> "Launching a revolution in the way consumers prepared meat and fish, *Shake 'N Bake* **was** first **introduced** in 1965. To cut down on preparation time and eliminate messy clean-up, the product included an envelope of seasoned coating mix for chicken or fish and a plastic shaker bag that could **be thrown** away after use."
>
> —*http://164.109.46.215/100/innovations/fasteasy.html*
> *Accessed May 26, 2004*

In this example, Shake 'n Bake is more important than Kraft, the company that introduced the product. And the disposable bag is more important than the cook who threw it away. These deliberate rhetorical choices show how decisions about language can support marketing strategies. Namely, this sentence emphasizes the product and one of its benefits—you don't have to wash the container!—rather than the company and potential customer.

Reason 3 for Passive Voice: The Writer Doesn't Know the Subject   Look at this example:

> In 1921, the first cargo of Clorox® bleach destined for store shelves in the Eastern United States **was loaded** aboard ship at the Port of Oakland.
>
> —*http://www.clorox.com/products/us_consumer'index.html*
> *Accessed May 27, 2004*

Certainly, I could revise the sentence this way:

> In 1921, **someone** loaded the first cargo of Clorox® bleach destined for store shelves in the Eastern United States aboard ship at the Port of Oakland.

Or:

> In 1921, workers loaded . . .

But we really don't know who did the loading. Besides, the subject—"first cargo of Clorox® bleach"—is more important in this context than are the souls who did the loading.
Let's take a look at one more example. This one comes from REI's guarantee:

> If any unauthorized charges **are** ever **made** to your card as a result of shopping here, you would pay nothing.
>
> —*http://www.rei.com/shared/help/returns.html?storeId=8000&stat=footer_100#guarantee*
> *Accessed May 27, 2004*

Because the writers don't know who might make those unauthorized charges, they've opted for passive voice.

Reason 4 to Use Passive Voice: Everyone Already Knows the Subject   When we talk about births, we typically put the receiver of the action—namely the child—in the subject. Consider this sentence:

I was born in November.

I certainly didn't have much to do with the bearing; my mother did all the work. But I'd never say, "My mother bore me." That's because everyone already knows that.

So now you have four rhetorical situations in which passive voice is OK. If you can't make one of these four arguments for using passive voice, you then need to know how to get rid of this construction. So let me take you through the steps.

First, look for all the forms of the verb "to be":

- Am
- Are
- Be
- Been
- Being
- Is
- Was
- Were

CAUTION: Have, had, having, have had, has, has had ARE NOT forms of the verb "to be."

Second, look at the next verb. If it looks like a past tense verb, you've probably got a passive construction. That part of speech is the "past participle." It's the **third column** in a conjugation:

1. Present	**2. Past**	**3. Past Participle**
Twist	Twisted	Twisted
Walk	Walked	Walked
Rise	Rose	Risen
Sink	Sank	Sunk

Usually, the past participle will look like a past tense verb. That's because most verbs in English are regular—that is, you just add an -ed to the end in both the past and past participle forms. You can see what I'm talking about by looking at the past and past participle forms in the words "twist" and "walk" above. However, irregular verbs throw a wrench into the formula—they'll end in -d, -en, -k, and -t, as "rise" and "sink" show. I don't know whom to blame for this annoyance.

Here's what we've got so far:

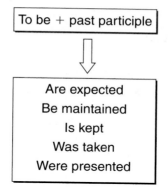

To be + past participle

⇩

Are expected
Be maintained
Is kept
Was taken
Were presented

Now let's look at a couple of these constructions in sentences:

All employees **are expected** to deal honestly with all others.

Company records must **be maintained** accurately.

A word of caution: An intervening word or two doesn't undermine the formula:

Using a "chill roll" apparatus that enabled hot cheese to quickly cool as it revolved over a cold drum, a sheet of cheese could **be** <u>uniformly</u> **sliced** into ribbons and then stacks of three-inch square cheese slices.
—*http://164.109.46.215/100/innovations/kraftdeluxe.html*
Accessed May 27, 2004

So now you have the formula for identifying passive voice: To be + past participle. How do you change it to active? First, you have to know the answer to this question: by whom or by what? The following sentence contains the passive construction "be updated." So I need to ask, "**updated** by whom or by what?" In this example, the answer to the question "by whom or by what?" appears in the "by" prepositional phrase.

The information contained therein may **be updated** . . . by **Motorola.**
—*http://phx.corporate-ir.net/phoenix.zhtml?c=90829&p=irol-intermediate*
Disclaimer prefacing the Investor Relations page
Accessed May 27, 2004

The answer to "updated by whom or by what?" is "by Motorola." That answer becomes the subject. So let's put "Motorola" in the subject position to get an active sentence:

Motorola may update the information contained therein.

Consider this sentence. It doesn't have an explicit "by" prepositional phrase. So you'll need to make one up:

False or intentionally misleading statements of any kind should never **be made.**

Again, this sentence doesn't have a "by" prepositional phrase. But we still have to ask the question "by whom or by what?" or more precisely, "**made** by whom or by what?" We could come up with multiple possible answers to that question because the sentence doesn't provide the answer: by you, by employees, by the company. To demonstrate, I'm going to choose "you":

You should never make false or intentionally misleading statements of any kind.

NOTE: In addition to putting the answer "by whom or by what" into the subject position, you have to keep the tense the same. And you get your clue about tense from the "to be" in the original passive sentence. Let's look at the original sentence one more time:

False or intentionally misleading statements of any kind should never **be** made.

Notice the "to be" verb. "Be" is the present tense. So in the revision, we need to maintain present tense:

You should never **make** false or intentionally misleading statements of any kind.

That's about everything you need to know (or ever WANTED to know) about passive voice. But let's review. To find passive voice, look for:

To be + past participle

Find the answer to the question "by whom or by what?" Put the answer in the subject position of the revision. Be sure to take the tense for the revised sentence from the "to be" in the original sentence.

   Bottom line: Use passive voice if you have a rhetorically sound reason for doing so. Otherwise, use active voice.

Plain English

Use plain English in your business writing. While this advice about writing sounds so simple, this strategy can be difficult for a number of reasons. First, many college professors value big words. Second, tests like the SAT, GRE, and GMAT include a verbal section, and scoring well on these tests requires a strong vocabulary. And finally, some segments of popular culture promote "a super powerhouse vocabulary" through self-help programs like Verbal Advantage®.

   But to write effectively for business audiences, you have to adopt strategies that maximize your readers' efficiency. Plain English is one such strategy. In fact, in the last 20 years or so, the plain English movement has significantly affected communication in government agencies, the health care industry, and the corporate world. When Bill Clinton was in the White House, he issued a Presidential Memorandum in 1998 requiring that plain English be used in federal documents. When Arthur Levitt was chairman of the Securities and Exchange Commission in the late 1990s, he instituted plain English requirements for all disclosure documents. Ford Motor Company revised leasing documents using plain English strategies and saw its leasing program become profitable. And GlaxoSmithKline uses plain English in literature that explains its clinical trials to patients.

Plain English simply means favoring the words you'd use in everyday conversation and using the technical jargon of your discipline when you have a good reason to do so. Or to put it another way, plain English means favoring single-syllable words over multisyllabic behemoth expressions. That's all. Plain English also means using personal pronouns and contractions. In applying plain English strategies, your reader gets a commonsense conversational tone.

Consider the following opening from a recent letter from Warren Buffett, head of Berkshire-Hathaway:

> Dear Reader,
>
> You probably know that I don't make stock recommendations. However, I have three thoughts regarding your personal expenditures that can save you real money. I'm suggesting that you call on the services of three subsidiaries of Berkshire . . .

Here, 29 of the 37 words are single syllable words.

Redundancies

Avoid repetitiveness, verbosity, wordiness, windiness, prolixity, circumlocution, and verbal effusion. Anyway, don't repeat yourself and don't qualify words or phrases unnecessarily. For instance, "large in size" is redundant because what else is "large" but a size? Or avoid "past experience" or "actual experience"—you can't experience something in the future, and you can't experience something if it doesn't exist. Style guides have lots of examples; I've just listed a few here:

Absolutely complete	complete
Basic fundamentals	fundamentals
Check up on	check
Disappear from sight	disappear
Each and every	each
Few in number	few
Hopeful optimism	optimism
Important essentials	essentials
Joint cooperation	cooperation
Mix together	mix
New innovation	innovation
One and the same	the same
Period of time	period
Repeat again	repeat
Same identical	same
Total of ten	ten
Unsolved problem	problem

Document Design Matters

If you think back to the 2000 General Election and Palm Beach County, Florida's "Official Ballot," you'll remember we almost had a constitutional crisis. Because election officials did a poor job of designing the now-infamous "butterfly" ballot, voters claim they were confused. If you take a look at the ballot below, you'll see why.

Democrats appear second in the lefthand column.

Democrats' vote hole appears third. So choosing the second vote hole is a vote for Pat Buchanan's Reform Party.

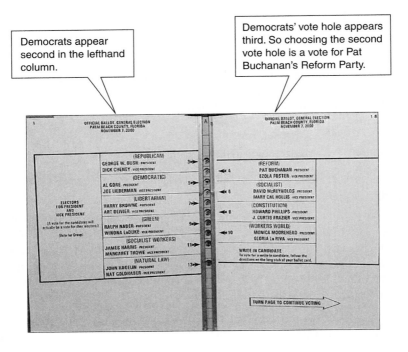

This design is a problem because it's confusing. So let's spend a little time addressing four key document design techniques. If you can apply these techniques, your business documents will be more effective and efficient for your readers.

The four document design techniques evident in effective business documents are:

{
- **H**eadings
- **A**ccessibility
- **T**ypography
- **S**pacing

Headings

You'll want to use headings in your document because they show both your document's organization and serve as navigational signposts for your readers. Specific headings announce the nature of the sections that follow.

To create effective headings:

- Be specific. A heading like "Results" doesn't do much. Rather, "Earnings are up this quarter" is a heading with more specific results.

- Consider using questions. Something like, "How were results last quarter?" implicitly promises your reader the answer in the ensuing section.

- Create a logical hierarchy of headings. All caps and bold might serve as a first-level heading for your main sections. All bold with a period might serve as a second-level heading. And bold with a period and text immediately thereafter might serve as a third-level heading. (See Exhibit 1 on page 28 for how these three heading options might look.)

Accessibility

When a document is accessible, it's easy to skim for the key ideas. Bulleted lists and numbered lists help make text accessible. But perhaps one of the most important tools you can use to make your text accessible is visuals—charts, graphs, maps, pictures, flow charts, and timelines, for example. You've head the age-old saying "A picture is worth a thousand words." That's why, in elementary school, we had "show and tell"—not just "tell."

As we moved through the educational ranks, we got lots of reading assignments. When the text included "pictures," I was happy. When I had to slog through the muck of dense paragraphs—relieved by nothing more substantial than a measly paragraph break—I was miserable. That's because interpreting the visuals was a more efficient process.

Now that you're older, what catches your eye first when you open a magazine? The pictures—in spite of the argument "I get that magazine for the articles." Sure, buddy.

---

[9] These four techniques come from William H. Baker, "HATS: A Design Procedure for Routine Business Documents." *Business Communication Quarterly* 64, no. 2 (June 2001), pp. 65–76.

Exhibit 1

Heading Options

HEADING [First Level]

Tas;dlfjsa;d lfjs l;fjd lsafj a;slfj afj alsfj ;fj salfjdlsjdfklsajfd;l jsflds jl;jsfkl asfjklsaj flks;flsafj a;alsfj ;alsfj fj fj; alsfjd las;flk jsafdjksld;fl jksa fjks;als fjd ajskfdl;lsa jdjksad;flkj ajaskfdl; lsajdf jsakl;alsfj jfk;alsfjd jfk;alsj.

T;asfdlkj sajdfkl; aslfj jsfkl;aslfj jfksl;alsjd fjls;alsfj jfkdls;lafjds jfkdls;alsfjd asd; lkj sajdfl ;saf jskf;lsa jdfjklads;lfk jsjdfkl;asjd fkls;afjl skl;af jksl;alsfjd jfksdl;afj fjskdl;alsjd jfksl;afj jsfkla;lsfjd sjkla;sfjkl sj;alfjjsdklas;dfljk sjfkla;sdfjkl fjskla;j sjfkla;sfjkl fjskd;afjk fjsla;sfjkl jsfk;a.

Heading. [Second Level]

Hasd;lkjs aas;fjkl sjdfkla;sfjk sjklsa;dl jsfl;jsalf wqpieuropw ujdlxcmv,./m asd;ofuwqois;adlfk as;df s,.df ds;fj ladj? ;aslfj sjdfl asd;fjkl sjfkl;asfj jskfdl;ajkl dfjk;alsfjd fjk;afjd fjs;alsf jfk;aljdsf sa;sfj jkls;a.

Heading. [Third Level] Yasdf;ljk jslas;flk as df ;lja sjdfkl; sjd jksd;afj fjs;afj fjk;afjd fj;alsjdf jsfk;af jksl;alsf fjks;afj fj;af jkfsd;a   pqeiuriweopqoweiurwe iop;qewu rjkld o2pa;dfjk dskjfl l93 ks;ml dsf jsd sdajf.

As; lk sd;fl jasdfl; lsfj jsfklqpoieu adsm xzc/mv am., msd,./vm a,.dms./f m.xcmv lk;jsa /,.cmvs;afjd ./,xcm vka;jfd a/,. Saoiuq;ldjas kljfkljdsf as;dlfj sjdka;sdlfjk jqklpodj a..

Heading. [Third Level] Dsf jfjklsad;fl jsd jkdfl;alsfjd jfs;aljds jfkdl;alkjdf quipewrouew q;kl lcmz vn xcnv nvx. ,zvn,mx.zx,cmnv nmx,.zx,cvn z., vm zx,cvn mxcv lakhd jkhjdsfla,.xcmvn kalhjd .zx,chvajk dlk hzxc,mhad,.vhxc lkad.

Heading. [Second Level]

Hasd;lkjs aas;fjkl sjdfkla;sfjk sjklsa;dl jsfl;jsalf wqpieuropw ujdlxcmv,./m asd;ofuwqois;adlfk as;df s,.df ds;fj ladj? ;aslfj sjdfl asd;fjkl sjfkl;asfj jskfdl;ajkl dfjk;alsfjd fjk;afjd fjs;alsf jfk;aljdsf sa;sfj jkls;a.

Hasd;lkjs aas;fjkl sjdfkla;sfjk sjklsa;dl jsfl;jsalf wqpieuropw ujdlxcmv,./m asd;ofuwqois;adlfk as;df s,.df ds;fj ladj? ;aslfj sjdfl asd;fjkl sjfkl;asfj jskfdl;ajkl dfjk;alsfjd fjk;afjd fjs;alsf jfk;aljdsf sa;sfj jkls;a.

And so on . . .

Bottom line: make your business prose accessible by incorporating reader-friendly visual breaks. Moreover, research is on your side here. According to some educational researchers, most of our learning occurs visually, as the chart below shows:

Learning and the Five Senses

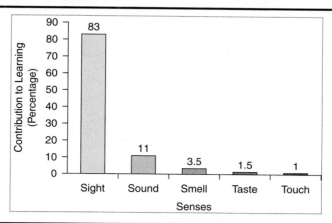

Source: http://www.osha-slc.gov/doc/outreachtraining/htmlfiles/traintec.html; accessed May 24, 2004.

Now consider the following finding. After just three days, businesspeople retain information much more readily when they both hear and see it. So add some artwork to your documents.

The Significance of Visuals on Information Retention

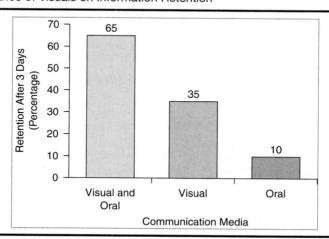

Source: http://www.osha-slc.gov/doc/outreachtraining/htmlfiles/traintec.html; accessed May 24, 2004.

Typography

In talking about "typography," I'm referring to font, type size, and typeface. So let's look at each.

Font   The font is really the design of the letters on the page. And fonts fall into one of two categories:

- Serif fonts—fonts with little feet like Century, Garamond, and Times New Roman.
- Sans serif fonts—fonts without (sans) little feet like Arial, Century Gothic, and Tahoma.

Here's how you decide which font to use. If your readers are going to read a "hard copy" document, use a serif font. Most newspapers, magazines, and books in this country use serif fonts. That's because the serifs have this interesting effect on readers—the serifs help readers' eyes move more easily from letter to letter and word to word. This "linking effect" allows readers to read more quickly.

If your readers are going to read an "electronic copy" document, use a sans serif font. When documents are projected electronically, the pixels do a better job at conveying crisp fonts when those pixels don't have to accommodate serifs. So for email and PowerPoint, use a sans serif font.

Type Size   Use 10-, 11-, or 12-point font. Here's my rule—the older the eyes, the bigger the font. So if you think your readers might be older than 40, use 12 point. Remember, in business, your readers will look for any excuse to stop reading. So don't let "I can't see this!" become one of those excuses.

Typeface   By typeface, I'm referring to various emphasis techniques like bold, underline, and italics. You'll have to find the right balance when using these techniques. If you use them too much, you'll lose the effect. And if you don't emphasize enough context, you'll lose the effect.

- _In this example,_ I'm using **_lots of different emphasis techniques_**. As a result, <u>too much</u> is **competing** for your attention, so **<u>not much</u>** gets your _attention_.
- In this example, I'm not emphasizing enough **context,** so I've significantly reduced your ability to skim this section.
- In this example, I want to emphasize this point: **find the right balance for emphasis techniques.**

Spacing

White space is good in business writing. That's because people don't like to read massive blocks of dense text. They want "text to be short and to-the-point," according to researchers John Morkes and Jakob Nielsen, who have conducted writing usability studies.[10] People like to read things that are broken up—it gets the point across more quickly.

Let your word processing software set the margin defaults 1 to 1½ inches. That should be fine for external spacing. And allow for space in between paragraphs and bulleted lists and visuals. Just let your eyeballs guide you. If the document looks good to your eyes—if the document looks like something YOU'D WANT to read—then trust your eyes.

---

[10] John Morkes and Jakob Nielsen. "Applying Writing Guidelines to Web Pages." January 6, 1998. http://www.useit.com/papers/webwriting/rewriting.html, accessed May 24, 2004.

2

Business Speaking Basics

Chapter Emphasis and Rationale

This section presents a general framework for putting a presentation together. Your specific purpose for speaking and your specific delivery style will—and should—deviate from this baseline framework.

   This chapter covers the following presentation topics:

- Managing the content by organizing it.
- Creating appropriate supplements.
- Delivering the content.

Managing the Content[1]

I'm going to address two aspects related to managing content: organizing your material and supporting your general claims.

Organizing Your Material

To organize your material in a meaningful way, you first have to know why you're talking. And to figure out for yourself why you're talking, you need to answer the question: "What do I want my audience to do or to know?" With that answer, you're ready to follow (and adapt as you need) the outline on the next page. (See page 32.)

   I need to make one additional comment with regard to the outline. You'll sometimes need to divide a main point into smaller subpoints. For example, a first point might focus on "Changes in Benefits" and could cover health insurance, annual and sick leave, and retirement. Given this information, the outline—just for this point—might look like the outline at the right.

Point 1: Changes in Benefits
• Insurance
• Subpoint 1 about insurance
• Subpoint 2 about insurance
• Etc.
• Leave
• Subpoint 1 about leave
• Subpoint 2 about leave
• Etc.
• Retirement
• Subpoint 1 about retirement
• Subpoint 2 about retirement
• Etc.

---

[1] See the chapter on "Business Writing Basics" for information about audience analysis and purpose statements. The information there applies to business speaking.

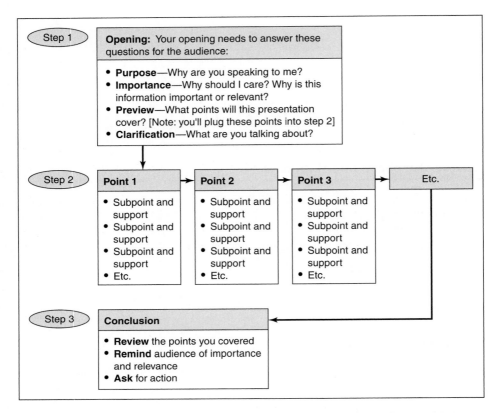

If I were going to deliver this information, I could include a secondary "introduction" for this section, which would include the elements of a main introduction as needed: purpose, importance, preview, and/or clarification.

Supporting General Claims

In addition to organizing your content, you need to include support for the general claims you make. Doing so makes you credible, and being credible makes you persuasive. You have a number of options to support your claims:

- Numbers and statistics
- Examples (history, consequences, anecdotes)
- Authorities on the topic

Let's look at each of these options, starting with **statistics.** In this excerpt from the Securities and Exchange Commission, the writer has used statistics to quantify (1) the number of shareholders, (2) the value of new securities, and (3) the number of securities that lost all their value.

Tempted by promises of "rags to riches" transformations and easy credit, most investors gave little thought to the dangers inherent in uncontrolled market operation. During the 1920s, approximately **20 million** large and small shareholders took advantage of post-war prosperity and set out to make their fortunes in the stock market. It is estimated that of the **$50 billion** in new securities offered during this period, **half** became worthless.

—U.S. Securities and Exchange Commission

http://www.sec.gov/about/whatwedo.shtml, accessed July 5, 2004

Using relevant examples can also provide support for general claims.

The length of time your broker must keep records depends on the type of record. **For example,** firms must retain blotters containing all purchases and sales of securities for at least six years.

—U.S. Securities and Exchange Commission

http://www.sec.gov/answers/bdrecrd.htm, accessed July 5, 2004

You can take several additional approaches when thinking about appropriate examples. For instance, taking relevant examples from **history** (broadly defined) is effective. The following text from Smuckers.com uses the company's history as a way to validate the company's current and future values.

Our Basic Beliefs are an expression of the values and principles that guide our Company's strategic behavior and direction. These basic beliefs are deeply rooted in the philosophy and heritage of the Company's founder, Jerome Monroe Smucker. Because he made a quality product, sold it at a fair price, and followed sound policies, the Company prospered.

Today, we continue to grow by adhering to our Basic Beliefs of quality, people, ethics, growth, and independence. These time-honored principles have served as a strong foundation throughout our history, and serve as the guideposts for all our future strategy, plans, and achievements.

—J. M. Smucker Company

http://www.smuckers.com/fc/about/ourbeliefs.asp?, accessed July 11, 2004

This example from Boeing also includes a bit of history. This history, however, shows the **consequences** of merging with McDonnell Douglas:

Boeing has been the premier manufacturer of commercial jetliners for more than 40 years. With the McDonnell Douglas merger in 1997, Boeing's legacy of leadership in commercial jets now is joined with the lineage of Douglas airplanes, giving the combined company a 70-year heritage of leadership in commercial aviation.

—The Boeing Company

http://www.boeing.com/companyoffices/aboutus/brief.html, accessed July 11, 2004

The phrase "With the McDonnell Douglas merger in 1997" conveys the consequence of the merger. If we look at that phrase a little more closely, here's the message it's sending: "The consequences of the result of the McDonnell Douglas merger in 1997 . . ." I'm not lobbying for a revision of the original—it's just fine. However, I do want you to see that the strategy this writer has used is one that shows the consequences of a particular act. And while this consequence is a good one, keep in mind that consequences can also be bad.

Anecdotes and **stories** also make effective examples. Somewhere I read that persuasion is 50 percent fact and 50 percent emotion. And that statistic makes sense. Think about the last time you bought something you really didn't need or really couldn't afford. The facts probably told you not to do it: you already have one (history); it's too expensive (statistics); your credit card balance will become unmanageable (consequences). In spite of all the facts NOT to buy it, your emotions won out: it makes me feel good; I deserve it.

That kind of thinking doesn't necessarily stop just because you put people in a business setting. Mind you, businesspeople are certainly interested in facts; however, they're also fundamentally human and will respond to emotional appeals when relevant, on-topic anecdotes and stories make those appeals real.

While you can find numerous, comprehensive books on storytelling, I want to give you a basic recipe.

Ingredients

- Take a basic situation.
- Stir in some challenges, problems, struggles, or trouble courtesy of the antagonist(s).
- Serve the results.

You're conveying information via the first two bullets as a way to then show how you prevailed over the bad stuff. When Indra Nooyi, CFO of PepsiCo, spoke at Tuck's School of Business at Dartmouth, she told the story of Pepsico's "dark clouds" in 1996. That year, Roger Enrico became CEO, and by year's end, the company had taken some fairly serious financial hits. To cap things off, *Fortune* pictured Enrico on its cover inside a Coca-Cola bottle.

Nooyi then talked about the specific strategies she, Enrico, and others at PepsiCo implemented. Then here's what she said:

> "In 2001, every PepsiCo operating division produced higher revenue and operating profit than the year before."
> —**Remarks by Indra Nooyi, September 23, 2002**
> *http://216.239.41.104/search?q=cache:RBhVbasyNpQJ:mba.tuck.dartmouth.edu/cgl/downloads/IKN-TUCK_.pdf+indra+nooyi+pepsico+tuck&hl=en, accessed July 12, 2004*

In this example, Nooyi's story follows the story recipe beautifully:

- Situation—PepsiCo faces dark clouds in 1996.
- Challenges—Antagonists appear as financial challenges and competition challenges (Coca-Cola).
- Results—The figurative sun comes out for PepsiCo in 2001 with financial successes.

So tell some stories to help you make your point.

Finally, **quoting** well-known, relevant **authorities** can contribute to your credibility and your persuasiveness. When I teach executives at the U.S. Postal Service, I like to quote Postmaster General William Henderson, who retired from that position in May 2001. While still postmaster general, Henderson visited my university, and I had a few minutes to talk with him, at which time he gave me his views on public speaking. He urged executives and managers to speak in public whenever the opportunity presented itself because public speaking was the best form of "self-advertisement." That is, public speaking was an effective vehicle that executives and managers could use for moving up a corporate ladder.

To this day, I like to quote Henderson when I teach public-speaking classes for the U.S. Postal Service because that quotation provides a persuasive rationale for those classes. And it really gets the attention of participants.

In talking about financial issues, I might incorporate references to or quotations from SEC Chairman William H. Donaldson. That kind of support would be powerfully persuasive, as his biography demonstrates:

> As SEC Chairman, Mr. Donaldson is the chief regulator of America's securities markets and the chief enforcer of America's securities laws.
>
> A graduate of Yale and Harvard Business School, and a Marine Corps veteran, Mr. Donaldson has spent more than 40 years at the highest levels of business, government, and academia. He was a co-founder and CEO of the international investment bank and stock research firm Donaldson, Lufkin & Jenrette; the founder of Yale University's School of Management, where he served as Dean and Professor of Management Studies; an Under Secretary of State in the Nixon Administration and later counsel and special adviser to Vice President Rockefeller; the Chairman and CEO of the New York Stock Exchange; and Chairman, President, and CEO of Aetna.
>
> —**U.S. Securities and Exchange Commission**
> *http://www.sec.gov/about/commissioner/donaldson.htm, accessed July 5, 2004*

In case you've forgotten, we've been talking about presentation content. And we covered how to organize and support information. Before we move on, I want to make one final comment. Everything I said about plain English in the section titled "Business Writing Basics" holds true here . . . but even more. That's because if you slip up and use some bureaucratic language when you write something, your readers—if they want to take the time—can re-read what you wrote. They can try to understand your meaning if they decide to put forth the effort to re-read it. However, when you're speaking, your audience can't decide to relisten to what you've said—they can't rewind you. They get one chance. So while you have their attention, you need to be sure you convey your ideas as clearly as possible. Plain English helps you do that.

Here's a blank presentation outline. You might want to make some copies and use them for your next few presentations until this approach becomes automatic for you.

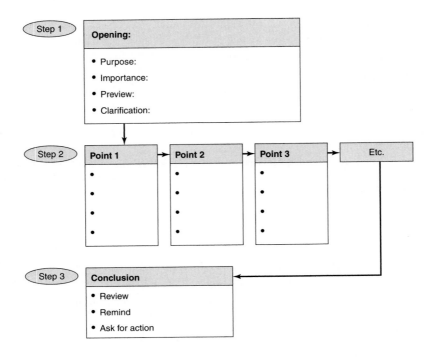

Creating Appropriate Supplements

When I refer to "supplements," I'm talking about the presentation extras—things like PowerPoint slides, handouts, and notes. So let's take a look at each one of these supplements.

PowerPoint

Love it or hate it—in business, you've got to use it because audiences expect it. So here are some highlights for using PowerPoint effectively.

1. **Use a sans serif font** like Tahoma, Century Gothic, or **Arial**. Electronically projected letters look sharper and stronger, and that subtlety sends a subliminal message that you, too, look sharper and stronger.

2. **Choose colors that contrast well.** When in doubt, project a prototype on a conference room screen, adjust the lights, and squint at the slide. If any text or visuals "melt" into the background, the contrast isn't strong enough. Don't rely on your laptop or desktop computer to check contrast:

   Colors always appear brighter
   Via pixels that are tighter.

   And pixels are "tighter" or closer together on desktop or laptop monitors.

3. **Keep your transitions and builds consistent** so your audience focuses on the message and not the "bells and whistles."

4. Be sure **bullets** are **grammatically parallel.** That is, start each bullet with the same part of speech.

5. Use a **consistent capitalization style.**

6. **Limit information** on slides; build timelines and processes as a way to control what your audience sees and when they see it; consider additional ways to transmit data-rich information. In other words, don't let PowerPoint's limitations limit what you want your audience to see. Supplement your slides with handouts.

7. **Incorporate visuals and charts.** For example, timelines can show project phases, maps put locations into relevant contexts, and schematics can show operational inefficiencies.

Handouts

Speakers often distribute hard copies of their PowerPoint slides so audience members can use the slides to add notes. However, consider creating handouts that enhance the "screen experience." For example, if you have complex financial data you need your audience to see so they're able to understand your points, include that complex information in a handout and then walk your audience through it. Don't throw that information up on a PowerPoint slide and say, "I know you can't see this information, but . . ." Instead, use the PowerPoint slide to convey the bottom line of that financial data and direct your audience to the handout.

Once you decide what to include in a handout, you need to decide when to hand it out. You have three options—before, during, and after. Here are the pros and cons of each:

*   **Before.** If you distribute your handout before your presentation, you minimize disruption, and audiences can take notes on the handout. However, you have to let your audience know how you want them to use the handout so they don't focus on it at the expense of listening to you. For example, you might say, "I'm sending around a handout that details some important financials; however, you don't need to look at it now. I'll let you know when we get to that section."

*   **During.** Distributing your handout during your presentation has one distinct advantage. You're able to hold the information until you're ready for your audience to see it. However, doing so takes time and can be distracting. So be sure to allocate time for the handout to get to everyone, and don't start talking until everyone has refocused.

*   **After.** Waiting until the end of your presentation to distribute your handouts has the distinct advantage of focusing your audience on you and giving you ultimate control over your information. However, you'll want to let your audience know you'll give them a handout at the end of your presentation with "such-and-such" information. At least they'll know they won't need to take copious notes, and they'll be thankful for that.

So decide which approach helps you best achieve your objectives, and distribute your handouts accordingly.

Using Notes

Notes are good. The business world moves much too quickly for us to cram every morsel of information into our overloaded brains. However, you'll need to integrate them naturally into your delivery. In other words, you don't want the notes to become a distraction to your audience. One of the absolute best techniques is to print your Power-Point slides (assuming you're using slides) with six slides per page and then fold the page lengthwise, as my diagram below shows. You'll have to augment those slides with your notes by hand, but it's an extremely elegant way to use notes during a presentation.

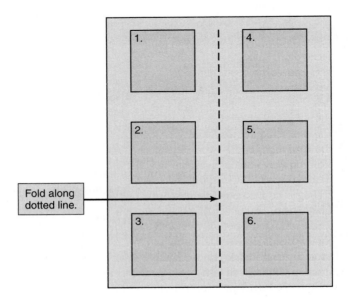

Delivering the Content

This part is important—that's because it's the part your audience sees. They don't see the hours of preparation; they just see you delivering your information. So if you want to be successful (and you do—otherwise, why put yourself through the stress?), you need to spend some time polishing your delivery skills. That is, you want to be sure "how you look" and "how you sound" enhances your content.

How You Look

Four categories related to "body language" impact your presentation style. They are:

- Eye contact
- Posture
- Movement
- Gestures

Eye Contact   While *you're* the center of attention during your presentations, audiences do want you to notice *them*. So look at them . . . ALL of them. Establish eye contact and maintain it. Don't look over their heads to the blank walls in the back of the room. Don't let your eyes dart like hummingbirds. Look at your audience . . . really look at them.

Be particularly sensitive to the audience facing your "exposed" shoulder when you're turning to look at your PowerPoint slides. Turn your head to them occasionally. Your body language will say to them, "I remember you're there, and you're important to me."

If you want to practice establishing good eye contact, try practicing the "X" pattern and "Z" pattern in an empty room until they become natural for you. The figure here shows you how this technique works.

X Pattern

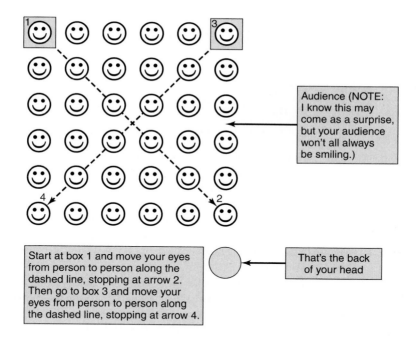

Z Pattern

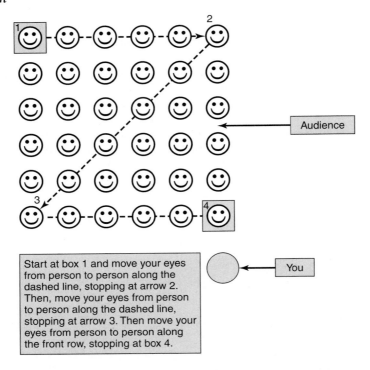

Audience

Start at box 1 and move your eyes from person to person along the dashed line, stopping at arrow 2. Then, move your eyes from person to person along the dashed line, stopping at arrow 3. Then move your eyes from person to person along the front row, stopping at box 4.

You

By using the "X" and "Z" patterns, you won't make eye contact with everyone in your audience. However, you will make eye contact with almost everyone. And that's pretty good! Oh, and just in case it's not clear, you need to move your head and neck when making eye contact . . . not *just* your eyes.

One last point about eye contact: don't look back at your projected PowerPoint slides unless you have a really good reason to do so. Your audience would rather see your "pie hole" than the back of your head as you shower them with information.

Posture   The way you carry yourself says a lot about how confident you are, and audiences take confident presenters more seriously than insecure presenters. While confidence can come in many forms, I'm going to share with you the baseline approach to exuding confidence: Stand up straight: keep your neck straight, your shoulders comfortably back, and your weight divided equally between both legs. A tilted neck conveys shyness. Droopy shoulders look sloppy. And weight on one leg makes you shorter, while sending the implicit message, "I really don't want to be here, and I don't care what you think." You don't want to appear shy, sloppy, or short.

I remember coaching a scientist who had spent 15 years working to increase the number of ears of corn on a single stalk. While the amount of arable land remains constant, the earth's population is growing exponentially. So how do you feed all those people? Well, you work to increase the yield of food per acre.

As I said, this scientist had spent a long time working on this challenge. As you might imagine, however, this notion of genetically modified food can get some people really angry. As just one example, people have ripped off their clothes in protest over genetically altered U.S. soybeans to, in their words, voice the "naked truth" about the "gene bean."

These kinds of reactions had, in my mind, affected this scientist's posture. As he presented the details of his research in the conference of his own company to his colleagues and manager, he tilted his head to the left, rounded his shoulders forward, and used the "palms-up gesture" (I talk more about "palms-up" in the section on "gestures"). Even though he distributed his weight equally between both legs, he looked like he might have been pleading with and ducking from imagined protestors. I told him to straighten his head and shoulders, adjust his palms, and deliver the same information again. The difference was astounding. His confidence—and executive presence—increased dramatically, all with the exact same information. So, your mother was right when she said, "Stand up straight."

Movement   You need to add a little visual interest to your presentation because—like it or not, fair or not—you're competing with the whiz-bang productions of television and movies. In that context, camera angles change every three to five seconds, and audiences sit comfortably with access to unlimited food and bathroom breaks. But in the context of business presentations, things just aren't as comfortable around a conference room table under the glare of fluorescent lights. So move. It adds visual interest and gets you out from behind any barriers.

Don't simply shift from side-to-side or heel-to-toe. That's just nervous energy seeping out. When you move, take controlled, full steps, and plant yourself in the new spot. To start, you may simply want to take two full steps toward your audience, make a few points, and then take two full steps back. The key to successful movement in front of a corporate audience is to control that movement.

Gestures   If you're going to "talk with your hands," just be sure your audience can see them. So gesture at waist level or above. Beyond that, you just need to observe these few simple techniques to have really strong gestures:

- Keep your wrists taut and your fingers relaxed. Doing so looks both confident and relaxed.

- Keep your hands apart, touching only your fingertips as if you feel a magnet pulling your hands together. Doing so makes you look open to your audience.

- Keep your palms slightly down or perpendicular to the ground. To show you what I mean, I want you to raise your palms (just your palms, now—not your arm and not your fingers) to the ceiling. That's what you'd do if you were pleading: "Mother, pleeeeeaaase let me go to see Jello wrestling this weekend."

- Move progressive gestures from your right to your left so your audience sees them from their left to their right. This technique reflects reading habits in which our eyes move left to right.

How You Sound

To be an effective presenter, you have to sound conversational. So never memorize a presentation, don't read your slides to the audience, and do create full-sentence, logical transitions that take your audience from one slide to the next. In other words, do not under any circumstances ever, ever, ever, read the title of your slide unless you work that title into a complete, natural-sounding sentence.

In terms of vocal quality, you need to consider four points:

- Inflection
- Pacing
- Volume
- Articulation

Inflection   When I talk about inflection, I'm referring to the change in pitch of a person's voice. It's really the counterpart to a monotone delivery. For example, your pitch might get lower (not in volume but in range) when you want to emphasize a point. Or inflecting up at the wrong time can affect the way people perceive your confidence. Consider *Jeopardy,* for example. Even though contestants provide answers in the form of questions, contestants who "down-inflect" at the ends of their answers sound much more confident.

So what should you do? Mimic a radio news broadcast. You can do so while you're in the car. In fact, I'm going to give you that advice for the other three points as well: **pacing, volume, and articulation.** Find your local NPR station—it broadcasts five minutes of news from the Washington, D.C., network headquarters at one minute past the top of every hour—i.e., 8:01, 9:01, 10:01, etc. Then parrot the news. If you do it enough, it will become automatic when you present.

Anxiety

I can't leave this section on delivery without addressing the issue of anxiety. Lots of people don't like to give presentations. However, you can adopt a few techniques— psychological and physical—to help you overcome this pesky nuisance. Let me say, however, that a little nervousness is a good thing—especially when it comes across as energy and enthusiasm.

Psychological Techniques during the Preparation Phase   After you've prepared your material, you can try visualizing your presentation. That's because your mind is incredibly powerful. It can't tell the difference between what is real and what it imagines clearly and vividly. Think about nightmares; they're not real. But when you wake up after one, you can still feel the physical sensations brought up by it. Or think about horror flicks. There you are . . . sitting in a darkened movie theater. The music is creepy and subdued. If you're like most people, your blood pressure will go up and your palms will perspire. But it's not real.

So how do you apply that concept to presentations? Imagine your presentation. I mean, really, really imagine your presentation. Close your eyes and imagine the room and its lighting; imagine the audience; imagine the opening of your presentation; imagine going through your data; imagine the Q&A; imagine the applause. You can easily make this exercise part of your preparation by imaging your presentation before you go to sleep at night or before you get up in the morning.

Physical Techniques before Presenting

Run and Present   My heart will sometimes race when I'm presenting, so I need to know how to control that sensation. You can replicate that sensation during your practice sessions if you elevate your heart rate. So . . . set up your presentation for practice and then run up a flight of stairs, down a hallway, or around the building[2] and back to where you set up your presentation and present immediately. You'll experience breathlessness and a racing heart, symptoms of nervousness. You'll find this exercise helpful because the feeling of nervousness won't be new to you when you present for real. As a result, you'll be better equipped to respond to those sensations.

Controlled Breathing   I like to control my breathing just before I give any presentation. It works well because no one sees you doing it, and it has the effect of slowing a racing heart. Simply inhale to the count of three or four, hold your breath for the same amount of time, exhale to the count of three or four, and hold your breath for the same amount of time. Repeat the sequence as often as you need. You'll love this technique!

Squeeze and Release   Isometric exercise can be good for reducing uncontrollable jitters. If your hands shake and you need to steady them, squeeze your forefinger and thumb together on each hand and hold as you count slowly to 10. Then release. You'll feel the nervous energy dissipate. In fact, you can apply this technique to any quivering part of your body. I once had a student give a practice presentation, and I wanted her to do it again. When she said, "But Professor Schultz, I'm so nervous my butt cheeks are quivering," I simply said, "OK, Suzanne, just squeeze and release." So squeeze and release.

Techniques during Your Presentation

During a presentation, the rules for the audience are different from the rules for you.

The Audience and Their Body Language   Your body language needs to be open, so don't cross your arms. On the other hand, your audience can cross its arms. However, that gesture doesn't necessarily mean they're closed to you and your ideas. The room might be cold; that posture might be more comfortable; they might be tired. In other words, interpret your audience's body language in a positive way unless explicit action from them indicates you should do otherwise.

---

[2] Of course, check with your doctor to be sure you're fit to do so, and don't trip.

The Audience and Their Eye Contact   You'll always find at least one "head-bobber" in the crowd. That's the person who is nodding affirmatively to the points you're making. Focus on that person or those persons first. That's what George W. Bush did in South Carolina when he ran in that state's primary for the Republican nomination for president in 2000.

The race was a tough one between George Bush and John McCain. But at each stop that Bush made, something interesting happened. Bush started each speech by looking at a woman just behind the crowd who was in the role of "head-bobber." Clearly part of the campaign, she smiled, nodded affirmatively, and clapped enthusiastically. And that's the person George Bush always looked at first. So if that's a technique good enough for the 43rd president of the United States, then it's a technique that's good enough for the rest of us.

I want to share just a couple of parting words. First, when presenting, you always look better than you feel. Finally, in a hundred years, we won't remember it anyway! Happy presenting.

S. N. Boyce and Its Catalog Division

Chapter Emphasis

• **Developing a Communication Strategy**

Rationale

Cell phones, voice-mail, email, instant messaging, Web sites, Web casts, conference calls, presentations, meetings, PDAs, letters, memos, and . . . oh, yes, face-to-face conversations—no wonder we suffer from information overload. According to a study by researchers at the University of California in Berkeley, each year we produce "roughly 250 megabytes [of information] for every man, woman and child on earth."[1] To put that number in some context, that equals about 150,000 pages of information for each person on the planet.[2]

We have so many ways to reach other people, and other people have so many ways to reach us. That's why having an effective communication strategy—one that recognizes not only the medium but also your audience, your credibility, your message, its organization, and its timing—is so important in today's workplace.

So how *does* one define "strategy"? It's a buzzword that businesspeople like to use to mean "plan." And it's important to have one for any important communication task. While you may be in the habit of "making it up as you go," this approach to business communication isn't effective or efficient. Here's why: As you communicate, your message passes through your audience's filter of biases, experiences, and knowledge. As a result, if you don't have a specific communication strategy, you increase the chances that your audience will misinterpret your message.

Because the purpose of any business message—whether oral or written—is to effect change and realize results—misinterpretation becomes costly, inefficient, and ineffective. So to minimize misinterpretation, this chapter provides the power of a communication

---

[1] Peter Lyman, Hall R. Varian, James Dunn, Aleksey Strygin, and Kirsten Swearingen. "How Much Information?" http://www.sims.berkeley.edu/research/projects/how-much-info/; accessed December 19, 2003.

[2] A 600-page book needs approximately 1 megabyte of ASCII storage.

strategy—a strategy you'll want to use throughout the book and throughout your business career. It then gives you the opportunity to apply the strategy to a business scenario.

Framework for a Communication Strategy

To begin formulating a communication strategy, you need to be familiar with four interdependent "constituents." The key word here is "interdependent" because each of these components affects and is affected by the others. They are:

1. **The subject/situation.**
2. **The communicator**—sometimes the writer, sometimes the speaker, but always YOU!
3. **The audience**—sometimes the reader, sometimes the listener, sometimes the spectators.
4. **The message.**

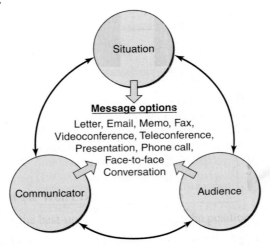

Taking inspiration from Aristotle's ethos, pathos, and logos and from Roman Jakobson's[3] communication triangle, I'd like you to look at how these four constituents work within a communication strategy.

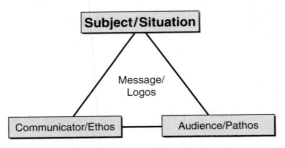

---

[3] Aristotle, *The Rhetoric and The Poetic of Aristotle*. Introduction by Edward P. J. Corbett (New York: McGraw-Hill, 1984). Roman Jakobson, "Linguistics and Poetics." In *Style in Language*. Ed. Thomas Sebeok (Cambridge, MA: The MIT Press, 1960), pp. 350–77.

The "Subject/Situation" in the communication triangle seeks to answer a number of "purpose" questions:

- What's your bottom line? Why are you communicating?
- What do you want your audience to know or to do?
- What do you want to accomplish as a result of this message?

In fact, you can answer the situation questions by completing this statement:

As a result of this message, I want my audience to _____.

Look at these examples:

- As a result of this message, I want my audience to understand the ordering procedures.
- As a result of this message, I want my audience to know about the cash settlement between Health Services, Inc., and ABC North America.
- As a result of this message, I want my audience to know we need to reevaluate our flagship brand strategy.
- As a result of this message, I'd like my audience to come to the 2004 National VP Marketing Meeting.
- As a result of this message, I want my reader to know I won't be extending an offer.

If you have time, glance through the mail you got today and find a business letter. You may have received a credit card solicitation, a renewal notice, or a magazine subscription solicitation. Look at the opening paragraph or two to find the author's purpose. As a result of that letter, what does the writer want you to do or to know?

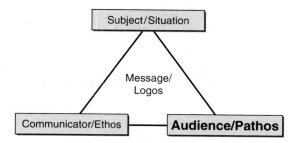

The "Audience" in the communication triangle seeks to understand audience complexities by answering these questions:

- Who's the audience? What's their attitude to the communicator, the situation, and the message? Is the audience open, closed, hostile, or something else?
- Do multiple audiences exist? (Primary, secondary, roadblock, or some other audience?)
- What's the audience's relationship to the communicator? (Insider, outsider, superior, subordinate, peer, or something else?)

While market research seeks to answer these questions in detail, "audience analysis" is typically more subjective for the day-to-day communication tasks most of us perform.

Still, your communication stands a better chance of succeeding when you understand that audiences can be complex, diverse, and differently motivated.

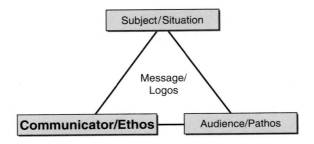

The **"Communicator"**—the writer or the speaker—in the communication triangle seeks to answer the following questions:

*   What's the communicator's level of credibility?
*   What's the communicator's relationship to the audience? (Insider, outsider, superior, subordinate, peer, or something else?)

Credibility is important because it affects the believability of your message. Some people such as Microsoft's Bill Gates, Harpo Entertainment's Oprah Winfrey, HP's Carly Fiorina, and Bank of America's Hugh McColl are credible because of who they are. They've built credibility from years of success. But what if you haven't yet established credibility based on who you are? You demonstrate credibility through messages that include appropriate, logical content, that reflect a professional appearance, and that avoid mistakes.

If you have time, take another look at that letter from today's mail. What's the writer's level of credibility? What position in the company does the writer hold? You may be able to determine the writer's position from the signature line. Is the letter free of mistakes? Does the writer provide support for claims made? In your letter, do these elements convey or undercut the writer's credibility?

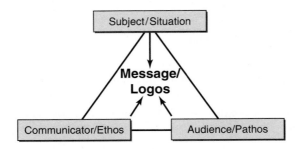

Once you understand (1) the "subject/situation" and what you want to accomplish as a result of the message, (2) to whom you're communicating, and (3) your role as the communicator, you're ready to make informed choices about the message. Specifically, the **"Message"** in the communication triangle seeks to answer the following questions:

- What's the best communication channel or medium for the message? (Letter, memo, email, presentation, conference call, voice-mail, Web cast, or something else?)
- What's the best timing? When should the message go out?
- Who gets the information, when, and in what form?
- What's the best organizational strategy? Direct or indirect? [NOTE: Because organizational strategies are much more complex than this, we'll address purpose statements (aka, "launches"[4]) and organizational strategies much more fully in the next chapter.]

So there you have it—a framework for approaching your communication tasks. Now I'd like you to apply this theoretical discussion to practice. Read the following scenario and take it through the steps of a communication strategy. You'll find the strategy questions at the end of the scenario.

S. N. Boyce's Background

After 137 years of continuous operation, the CEO of S. N. Boyce has made the difficult decision to close the company's catalog division and stop publishing the annual phone-book-sized "Boyce Book."

After S. N. Boyce founded the company in 1868, the catalog played a key part in the company's development. Farmers on the Great Plains and frontiersmen in the Old West eagerly awaited the annual publication, which increased from a 24-page booklet in 1870 to a two-pound catalog in 1893. The famous publication evolved into a well-known piece of Americana.

In the 20th century, shopping with the Boyce Book was a popular pastime among housewives in America's growing cities. Even though hundreds of downtown stores opened around the country by this time, many women who were busy at home rearing children preferred to shop by telephone. Throughout the early and mid-20th century, just about every household in the country had a Boyce Book on its bookshelf.

But by the late 1970s, catalog sales had begun to slow down. Shoppers were more mobile, stores stayed open later, and people had less interest in shopping by phone. Moreover, consumers who still preferred to shop by catalog had many new alternatives. Specialty catalog retailers such as Lands' End and L.L. Bean began to cut seriously into S. N. Boyce's sales.

In the past few years, competition from Web-based retailers (like the behemoth on-line retailer, Amazon, and even the company's own site—www.Boyceonline.com) have

---

[4] I am indebted to my colleague extraordinaire, Lynn Setzer, for this wonderfully descriptive term.

hurt catalog sales even more. And the company's market research shows most of the remaining catalog customers are people older than 50 who have been loyal S. N. Boyce shoppers for decades.

Since 1982, the S. N. Boyce catalog division has been losing money. Losses last year totaled $16 million. Though S. N. Boyce remains profitable overall, the catalog division has pulled down the value of the company stock. Wall Street analysts have been begging the company for years to shut down its catalog operation because of its "negative drain" on earnings. However, company leaders have been hesitant to abandon this veritable part of the organization.

Finally, after years of internal discussion, the CEO of S. N. Boyce has decided to end catalog sales. The company will not publish its Boyce Book next year, and it will accept orders only until the end of the current quarter. In return, the company expects this decision to have a positive effect on profits and earnings by the end of the next fiscal year.

The catalog division employs 52 people. Ten of them work at corporate headquarters. The rest are spread around the country at six regional distribution centers. (Exhibit 1 shows the company structure.) The company will offer some employees other jobs, but approximately 40 of the 52 employees will be laid off, and S. N. Boyce will sell the distribution centers.

Your Role

You are S. N. Boyce's CEO. Now that you've decided to close the catalog division, you'll have to communicate your decision.

Your Task

To formulate a communication strategy, answer the following questions thoughtfully:

1. What do you want to accomplish as a result of your message?
2. Identify all potential audiences. What is their relationship to you? How will they likely react to your information?
3. Analyze your level of credibility with each of the audiences you identified.
4. What is the best communication medium for each audience? (Letter? Memo? Email? Presentation? Phone call? Something else?) What timing issues should you consider? (Does everyone get the message simultaneously?)

Additional Tasks

1. Craft a message to Boyce employees.
2. Craft a message to the Board of Directors.
3. Craft a press release for the company Web site.

Exhibit 1

S. N. Boyce General Company Structure

The CEO, the executive staff, and administrative staff work at company headquarters. In addition, 10 catalog employees work there, while six employees—including a center manager—work at each distribution center.

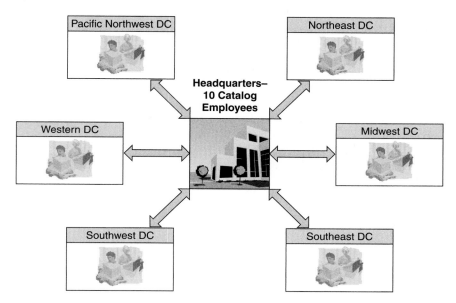

4

Wake Partners—The "New Conservative Mutual Fund"

Chapter Emphasis

- **Document Design**
- **Information Synthesis**
- **Informative Message Organization**

Rationale

Document design matters in business. That's because busy businesspeople will make any excuse to stop reading. If a document doesn't look inviting—if you haven't designed your message with "reading efficiency" in mind—you'll lose your readers. I promise.

Let me show you the first paragraph of a 1,322-word email message—you don't need to read it; just look at it:

> When I wrote to you at the end of February, I indicated that we needed to take another look at the challenges we face in today's marketplace. To that end, the HRO had the painful task of downsizing our staff by 23%. We also looked for numerous ways to reduce other expenses while maintaining our focus on customer service. Now, we are working on the new CCBM framework to change the way we sell our products. We've been heavily involved in distinguishing between our "flagship" and "specialty" brands. Given the reality of today's marketplace, however, we need to change how we market these brands. To help us on this path, you will recall that we announced the new Brand Focus Team (BFT). I asked one person from each brand to serve on this team. And I gave them the task of looking for more growth and a better way to allocate resources—no small task. As we look to more growth and profitability, we want to ensure a win-win

situation for our shareholders, our customers, and ourselves. So again, that's why we need to raise the bar and re-evaluate our strategic marketing plan. I know we have a lot of work ahead, but I want to give you some background information about what's going to happen here in the next few weeks. You'll get a 50-question survey called the "IWKWYT" survey that asks for your input. I want you to feel free to share all your ideas. I want to know what we can do better. All responses will be anonymous—you have my word. So please be honest. We'll tabulate the results and share them at the BFT meeting at the end of the month. After that, a team member from the BFT will be contacting you for one-on-one talks. They'll then ask you to participate in a 2-hour meeting to brainstorm some ways for re-positioning and marketing those brands and also share with you the results of the survey. I could say more about my ideas for how we need to proceed, but I won't do that—I want to hear from you. In anticipation of your much-needed participation, I want to say thank you. We wouldn't be where we are today without your hard works and dedication.

Would you believe that this message goes on for another 1,000 words or so? It does. Now be honest—does this email message look like anything you'd want to read? The text looks like a big uninviting blob to my eyes, so I'm not inclined to read it. Granted, we sometimes have to read messages like this one because of who wrote them, but most of us don't like it. And the implications are significant: If you want your readers to read your business messages, you'll need to design those messages to be inviting to your readers' eyes.

So how do you do that? You do that through HABITS, a structural design approach that includes

- **Headings** that show a logical organization in the document;
- **"Artwork"**[1] that shows and emphasizes ideas through both visuals and formatted lists;
- **Bold, Italics,** and **Typeface** that emphasize key ideas and enhance reading speed;
- **Space** that invites—doesn't overwhelm—your reader.

Let's look at each of these ideas in more detail.

Headings

When headings work well, they serve as mini internal "bottom lines." That is, the headings should give your reader a snapshot of what that section contains. The following letter from Social Security makes my point:

---

[1] I am again indebted to my colleague Lynn Setzer, for this wonderful descriptor for nontextual information.

Date

Recipient's Name
Recipient's Address
Recipient's City, State, and Zip Code

Dear Recipient:

This letter contains **Important Benefit Information.**

On July 16, we will deposit a special one-time Social Security benefit payment of $37.00 into your account.

Why a special payment?

Each year, you get a cost-of-living increase in your Social Security benefits. This increase is based on the consumer price index, or CPI. The CPI is the government's measure of the rate of inflation. In 1999, there was an error in how the CPI was figured. Because of this, Congress passed a law that allows us to make special payments to compensate for the shortfall. This special payment is for the benefits you would have received from January 2000 until now if the CPI error had not occurred.

What about future benefits?

We have reviewed all Social Security accounts and made changes if needed. Because the CPI error was so small (one-tenth of 1 percent), your regular monthly benefit amount may not have increased. Beginning in August, you will receive $1141.00

What if you disagree?

If you disagree with any of these amounts, you should write to us within 60 days from the date you receive this notice.

What if you have questions?

If you have questions, we invite you to visit our website at www.ssa.gov on the Internet to find general information about Social Security. You also can call us **at 1-800-772-1213.** We can answer specific questions by phone from 7 a.m. until 7 p.m. on business days. If you are deaf or hard of hearing, you may call our TTY number, 1-800-325-0778. You can also visit your local office.

> DUKE FOREST BLDG
> 3308 CHAPEL HILL BLVD
> DURHAM NC

Larry G. Massanari
Acting Commissioner of Social Security

012724041053

These headings are effective because they're specific. General headings don't shed any light on what a section contains. If you see the heading "Recommendation" in a document, you have no idea what the writer recommends. However, if you see "Change Flagship Brand Strategy," you're immediately clear on what the writer recommends. If your heading appears as a question, it implicitly promises that the answer and details follow in the text. So make your headings specific.

You also need to create a "heading template" that shows main level, first level, and second level headings for your document. I like this template:

MAIN SECTION

First Level Heading

Interesting text insightful text meaningful text critical text intelligent text original text thought-provoking text. Interesting text insightful text meaningful text critical text intelligent text original text thought-provoking text. Interesting text insightful text meaningful text critical text intelligent text original text thought-provoking text.

Second level heading   Interesting text insightful text meaningful text critical text intelligent text original text thought-provoking text. Interesting text insightful text meaningful text critical text intelligent text original text thought-provoking text.

Second level heading   Interesting text insightful text meaningful text critical text intelligent text original text thought-provoking text. Interesting text insightful text meaningful text critical text intelligent text original text thought-provoking text.

First Level Heading

Interesting text insightful text meaningful text critical text intelligent text original text thought-provoking text. Interesting text insightful text meaningful text critical text intelligent text original text thought-provoking text. (And so on . . .)

My template isn't the only one, and it certainly isn't the best one. It's just one that works for me. You, too, should come up with a template that works for you—that shows the overall relationship of the sections in your document.

Artwork

Which of the following examples would you prefer to see in a business document?

Example 1   I've put on 20 pounds in the last 8 years. In 1997, I weighed 127; in 1998, I weighed 130; in 1999, I weighed 132; in 2000, I weighed 133; in 2001, I weighed 135; in 2002, I weighed 140; in 2003, I weighed 143; in 2004, I weigh 147. Ugggg.

Example 2   I've put on 20 pounds in the last 8 years.

Year	Weight (in pounds)
1997	127
1998	130
1999	132
2000	133
2001	135
2002	140
2003	143
2004	147

Example 3   I've put on 20 pounds in the last 8 years.

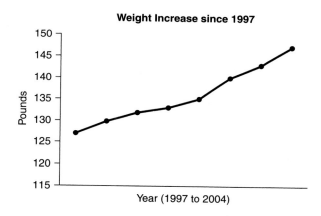

I don't like any of the examples because of the story they tell. That aside, most businesspeople prefer example 3 because that example allows them to digest the information most quickly. In other words, it *shows* the trend, thereby minimizing the level of mental acrobatics a reader must perform. (I need to perform some physical acrobatics—I'm going on a diet!)

Think of yourself as an information engineer. That way, you'll consider options other than text when designing your documents.

Message	Artwork Options
Chronological lists, process lists	Numbered lists
Other lists	Bulleted lists
Organizational charts	Flow charts
People, places, things	Pictures and maps
Project target dates	Time lines
Processes	Flow charts

Bold, Italics, and Typeface

Use the "bold" and "italics" function to emphasize your key ideas. However, don't overuse the techniques—doing so will have the opposite effect. Take a look at the end of this email message. I've presented it four ways to make my point:

No emphasis techniques:

To be eligible for one of our prizes, take the HR quiz. It's available online at http://hro.corp.acme/quiz. Then email your answers to HRO@corp.amce.com no later than 5:30 PM, Monday, August 2. The first 25 respondents to answer all the questions correctly win!

Not enough context:

To be **eligible** for one of our *prizes,* take the HR **quiz.** It's available *online* at http://hro.corp.acme/quiz. Then email your **answers** to HRO@corp.amce.com no later than 5:30 PM, Monday, August 2. The *first* 25 **respondents** to answer all the **questions** correctly win!

Too much context:

To be eligible for one of our prizes, take the HR quiz. It's **available online at http://hro.corp.acme/quiz.** Then **email your answers to HRO@corp.amce.com** no later than **5:30 PM, Monday, August 2.** *The first 25 respondents to answer all the questions correctly win!*

Just enough context:

To be eligible for one of our prizes, **take the HR quiz.** It's available online at http://hro.corp.acme/quiz. Then email your answers to HRO@corp.amce.com no later than 5:30 PM, Monday, August 2. The **first 25 respondents to answer all the questions correctly win!**

In the last example, I wanted to accomplish two goals: (1) I wanted to emphasize what I want the readers to do. That is, I want them to take the quiz. (2) I also wanted to make sure the readers saw the motivating factor: the incentive. So that's why I made the rhetorical choices I did. The figurative line between not enough context and too much context is a fine one. Just make sure you have a rhetorically sound reason for the choices you make.

In addition to using emphasis techniques, you need to make some choices about typeface. First, choose between 10-point and 12-point font because most people are comfortable with that size. Just one word of caution: The older the eyes reading your document, the larger the type size. So if your audience is 40 or over, go with 12 point. If your audience is younger than 40, 10 point should be fine.

Second, choose a "serif" typeface for any printed document. A serif typeface has little feet on the ends. It's an old printing convention that helps a reader's eyes move smoothly from letter to letter and word to word. In fact, if you pick up any newspaper or book, you'll notice the text has those little feet. That's because around 90 percent of printed documents in the United States use a serif font. You'll see the little feet on typefaces like Times New Roman, Book Antiqua, Garamond, and others.

On the other hand, if you're designing an electronic document—an email message, a PowerPoint presentation, or a Web page—pick a sans[2] serif font. Century Gothic (my current favorite for PowerPoint slides), **Arial**, and **Tahoma**, for example, are examples of sans serif fonts.

Space

Leave enough of it on the page. People want to read documents that provide visual relief, and space does just that. Break paragraphs that look too long, use bulleted lists, and insert visuals. I should tell you that lots of information is available about appropriate margin size, for example. However, the notion of spacing boils down to this for me: Trust your eyeballs. If the document looks inviting to your eyes and you've made informed choices in designing it, then it will look inviting to your readers' eyes.

I have one more point I want to make about space. As readers, we've grown accustomed to seeing a uniform space between words. For example, look at the space between words in this book. They're even. If we play around with alignment options in word processing software, we'll have multiple options: left align, centered, right align, and full justification. If you chose full justification, the spacing between words will be uneven. Unless you want to play around with complicated settings and options in your software to ensure even spacing between words, remember this advice: **Left justification is always your best choice.** Left justification ensures that spacing between words is consistent and even. And left justification gives your reader a consistent starting point for each heading, line, and paragraph.

So now, I'd like to give you an opportunity to apply some of the design concepts I just covered in this chapter.

Scenario Rationale

Early and often in your careers, your supervisor will ask you to gather, synthesize, and present information. This assignment gives you the opportunity to do just that: gather, synthesize, and present. *Please note: This assignment offers a simplified "finance scenario," which deliberately avoids financial theories, concepts, and decision models.*

The Situation

Wake Partners is an investment firm specializing in mutual funds. At the end of the next quarter, Wake Partners plans to offer its clients a new fund.

Your Audience

Your audience is Avery Polk. He's a senior analyst with Wake Partners, and Onslow Nash, the company's CEO, has asked Avery to select stocks for the company's new

---

[2] In French, *sans* means "without." Frederick the Great named his splendid home in 18th-century Potsdam "Sans Souci"—"Without Care." So "sans" serif means "without" serif . . . without feet.

fund. To make his decision, Avery needs information about the stocks he's considering, and he's asked several junior analysts to provide that information.

Your Role

You're a junior analyst with Wake Partners.

Your Task

Avery has asked you to gather information about a specific stock. (Please note: your instructor will assign the stock you need to research.) You'll need to provide information that answers the following two questions:

1. How has the stock performed during the last year? Get the stock's closing price for today, six months earlier, and a year ago. You may want to visit http://finance.yahoo.com to gather this information.

2. What has the CEO said about the company's performance and its stock in the most recent "Letter to Shareholders"? You should be able to find this information by going to the company's Web site, selecting the "investor relations" section, and selecting the most recent annual report.

Don't make a recommendation about whether Avery should include this stock in the new fund; simply convey the information he's requested.

Because you're writing an informative message, you'll want to consider organizing your document this way:

Start with an opening that considers the context and incorporates that context into a launch that includes the bottom line. Follow the bottom line and launch with appropriate details, explanations, and clarifications. Finally, end the message with a positive forward-looking close. For more information on how to organize informative messages, see the section in this book on "Message Types."

Nuts and Bolts

- Clarify your purpose.
- Synthesize the information in a memo addressed to Avery.
- Follow the organizational strategies for an informative message.
- Consider options for an effective layout.
- Limit your memo to one page.

It Has Come to My Attention . . .

Chapter Emphasis

- **Tone in Business Communication**
- **Organizing a Negative Message**

Rationale

My mother has a saying: The tone makes the music. As with music, tone can be positive, pessimistic, or poignant. Simply put, tone affects the way a message "sounds," so it affects a message's meaning. For example, if I say, "You look nice today" in a tone that's "matter-of-fact," you should take me at my word. But if I attach a sarcastic tone, you'll interpret my words differently.

In business messages, tone—the way a writer sounds on paper—is particularly powerful because it can convey both positive and negative images. Consider the tone in the following excerpt from a Corporate VP saying good-bye to employees affected by a division closure:

> This is a bittersweet time for us all as we say farewell to our friends and colleagues. Through good times and bad times, you've demonstrated professionalism, diligence, and resilience. I want to personally thank you for your contributions. You have tons to be proud of. You've made a huge difference for this company, our customers, and shareholders.

How would you describe the writer? Appreciative? Respectful? Here's an executive who clearly values her employees, and you can sense that simply from the tone of the message.

A few years ago, I flew to Washington, D.C., to do some communication consulting. Next to me sat the head of a national health organization who talked about the "tight ship" she ran. And I remember one thing in particular she said: "It's my way or the highway." I only remember this rather unoriginal cliché because later into our half-hour conversation, she mused, "I have a lot of turnover here."

I was surprised that she didn't make the connection between those two statements. Indeed, she struck me as an executive with blinders, someone closed to the strengths that employees can bring to an organization.

Unfortunately, however, she's not an anomaly in today's workforce. According to one survey, 81 percent of employees describe their supervisor as a "lousy manager."[1] In general, these ineffective bosses:

- Don't involve employees in decision making.
- Are rude and intimidating to employees.
- Endorse the "my way or the highway" theory.

If you're unlucky enough to work for a manager like this, you'll most likely find yourself on the job market sooner than you like. Towers Perrin, the New York City–based human resources consulting firm, commissioned a study[2] that found 28 percent of disgruntled employees are already job hunting. This statistic is a costly one. Indeed, this finding comes with a hefty price tag if you add the unquantifiable loss of intellectual capital to the financial cost of replacing a worker.[3]

The following excerpts from email messages show why so many employees are unhappy with their managers.

- This boss decided to pull the plug on microwaveable popcorn: "Eighty percent of all fire alarms in office buildings are because some idiot let it [popcorn] burn in the microwave. Last night we had another incident. . . . If you must have popcorn, buy it already made in a bag or a tin. If you have microwave popcorn at your desk, you will be terminated............Period! Thank you." Hmmm . . . nicely seasoned comments.

- Frustrated because some employees were helping themselves to meals designated for clients, this manager wrote, "It has come to our attention that some food was stolen out of a refrigerator in this building last week. . . . Please note, as was stated in the last food theft situation, if an employee is caught stealing food, his/her employment could be terminated."

- Here's a manager who was annoyed because employees weren't using the proper facilities: "It has been brought to my attention by Management that the 19th floor toilets are being used by staff. May I remind you all that these toilets are for the exclusive use of Guests and Visitors. There are sufficient toilet facilities available between floors 18 and 1. Use those."

- Here's a twist on the message above. In this case, this manager was annoyed because employees weren't using the facilities properly: "It appears that I have to remind a few people about things that should and should not take place in our restroom facilities: 1. Paper towels DO NOT go in the toilets. . . . 2. Feminine products DO NOT go in the toilets. . . . 3. Sinks are for washing hand, NOT HAIR. . . . 4. And lastly . . . if you see someone causing a mess in the facilities, or if you yourself happen to have a 'problem' and cause a mess, please inform me or my staff as soon as possible so that we can take care of it."

---

[1] Gordon Miller, "So Few Good Bosses, So Many Frustrated Employees." www.jobs.net/resources/candidates/general_articles/few_good_bosses.html, accessed May 13, 2004.

[2] "Working Today: Exploring Employees' Emotional Connection to Their Jobs," 2003, p. 7.

[3] Miller estimates that cost at $36,000.

- Here's a messy situation this manager had to confront: "There is an issue going on in the men's bathroom. . . . This is the second time that we found s---all over the floor. . . . Also, somebody has been socking rolls of tissue in the toilet. . . . This has to STOP. . . . I am enclosing the names of the people who were in the store at the time of the incident."

- This manager wanted everyone to work together. Take a look at this excerpt: "We aren't f---ing kidding about everyone answering the phones. This is part of our culture. If you think this doesn't apply to you, don't make any large cash purchases any time soon. . . . We sent out a nice email about this. Apparently it didn't work. This ain't no disco, this ain't no party, this ain't no fooling around. I f---ing mean this."

- Safety is important in the workplace, and this manager took that notion seriously: "Today there was another rubber band shooting occurrence. I want to remind you all that this is not acceptable behavior at work. Since I don't know who's shooting the rubber bands, I am going to put a copy of this email into each of your personnel files. Since this is not acceptable behavior, if it continues, it will result in penalty."

- Here's a manager committed to creating an efficient workplace: "It has come to my attention that several employees are talking at their desks during scheduled work hours. I must convey the importance of NOT talking at your desk or to your desk partner. Talking greatly decreases work productivity and company morale. . . . We want you to work hard and enjoy your work. Please contact management if you have any questions."

Would you want to work for any of these managers? I didn't think so. These missives from managers generate negative emotions in the employees who work for them. And because you don't want to BE any of these managers, I thought you'd find it interesting to learn that the Towers Perrin study I mentioned above tracked a "statistically significant" correlation between positive employee emotion and a company's "bottom line."[4]

It boils down to this: People want to believe they matter to a company. Consider this voice-mail message Goldman Sachs CEO Henry Paulson sent to his employees: "Our assets will always be our people, capital, and reputation, with our people being the most important of the three. . . . And the lesson here is that our principles will never fail us as long as we do not fail to live up to them."[5] When 9/11 happened, Paulson's employees pulled together and pulled through because, in their minds, they mattered not only to Goldman Sachs but also to Paulson.

Building a corporate culture based on mutual respect requires positive communication. But it also requires two-way, open communication. When Fred Hassan took over as CEO of Schering-Plough in May 2003, he was given the task of fixing the giant drug maker's problems in the lab, in the plants, and in the market. To accomplish this task, he instituted "talk therapy" and initially brought together 11 midlevel researchers. He wanted to know, from their perspective, the challenges facing Schering-Plough. From these and other conversations, Hassan has learned that "speed" is a bad word and that

---

[4] "Working Today: Exploring Employees' Emotional Connection to Their Jobs," 2003, p. 10.

[5] Paul Argenti, "Crisis Communication: Lessons from 9/11," *Harvard Business Review* (December 2002), p. 8.

the internal route to FDA approval has been long, arduous, and demoralizing. While change will most likely be slow, Hassan is already getting credit from his employees for opening up the communication channels.[6]

To help you define your own effective management communication style—even when you need to communicate negative information—I'd like you to answer the following questions and be prepared to discuss them in class. After answering and discussing the questions, move on to the assignment.

Questions

1. Characterize the writer in each of the excerpts above. Would you want to work for any? Defend your answer.

2. Is the tone justified by any of those writers?

3. Could plain English improve the tone of each? Would plain English be appropriate? Why or why not?

4. Should the writer incorporate personal pronouns and contractions? Why or why not?

5. What specific characteristics define an effective communicator?

6. How do those characteristics change—if at all—when the communicator is a manager and has to convey bad news?

7. If you need to convey bad news to employees, what communication channels should you consider? Why?

8. In the excerpts, have any of the writers chosen the correct communication channel? Why or why not?

Organizing Negative News

Writing a negative message has its own challenges because no one likes getting bad news. So consider cushioning the "blow" of bad news with a short "context statement." For example, you might begin a rejection letter this way: "Thank you for applying for the Consulting Internship here at ABC." Or tell your manager something good before moving on to the negative information. Look at this example: "While enthusiasm on the sales floor shows a real passion for what we sell, I've seen us lose sales because the noise level doesn't give our customers the level of concentration they need."

If, however, your negative news doesn't affect the reader directly or personally or if you want to save time and your "executive persona" values directness, then you may eliminate the cushion. Just be clear on why you're including or excluding the cushion.

The negative information should come relatively early in the document. It's your bottom line—your reason for writing. Say it, don't dwell on it, don't repeat it, and move on to your reasons, explanation, and/or details. Your readers will need the reasons so they can put the bad news into some kind of meaningful context. Why aren't you hiring me? Give me the reasons. Why aren't we getting raises this year? Give me the reasons.

---

[6] John Simons, "Is It Too Late to Save Schering?" *Fortune* (September 15, 2003), p. 145.

Why should we be concerned about the noise levels on the sales floor? Give me the reasons. Sometimes, the bad news and the reasons will appear in the same sentence: "We won't refund your money because your receipt is over 30 days old." If your reasons then need clarification—and often they will—provide the details you believe your readers need so they understand the reasons.

Once you've covered these elements, move on to a positive close. "I wish you well in your job search." "Let me know if you have questions about this decision." "I hope the next fiscal year brings a budget that rewards the hard work you've done." "While I understand this news isn't what you had hoped for, thank you for raising your concerns with ABC company."

One word of caution: These elements—*cushion, bad news, reasons, explanation/details, and positive* close—should unfold in a logical manner. In other words, sometimes the reasons will come before the bad news. Sometimes, the bad news will appear in the first sentence. Sometimes, the cushion won't fill a useful role. So use these elements to *guide* you, and tweak them as you see fit.

Assignment

Assume you and your classmates work for the same division within a company—you as the manager and your classmates as your direct reports. As manager, you've identified a negative situation or event that you need to address to your employees. Perhaps some employees are arriving consistently late to work; perhaps employees are spending too much time writing personal email messages; perhaps employees aren't recycling as much as they should be. Consider other negative situations.

Understanding the effects that a negative tone can have on morale and profits, develop a message to address the problem. You'll find completing the following prework useful for establishing a context:

1. Describe the company. What do we do? What do we make?

2. Describe your purpose. Why are you writing? What do you specifically want to accomplish as a result of your message?

3. Describe your audience. What is your specific relationship to your audience? Consider your primary audience and secondary audience. Do you need to consider other audiences?

4. What's the best communication channel or medium or media? Email? Division meeting? Why?

5. If you decide you need to convey your bad news via a memo or email message, draft the message.

6

Payroll's Paperless Payday

Chapter Emphasis

- **Structuring the Informative Message**[1]
- **Communicating with Employees**
- **Using Technology in the Workplace**

Rationale

For employees to work effectively, they need information. They might, for example, need to be familiar with the expectations and steps for making a successful sales call, or they might need to understand the procedures for ordering supplies, or they might need to know how to operate equipment. Indeed, "informative messages" aren't just *common* in the workplace; they're *essential* to a company's operational success.

To that end, this chapter gives you the tools you need to write an effective informative message.

As a first step, anytime you want to convey information, you need to decide exactly what you want your audience to know. What information do they need? At this point, you don't need to worry about "why" they need the information. You just need to worry about "what" information they need. Make sure this distinction is clear in your mind. If you're crystal clear on "what" you want your audience to "know," then you're ready to articulate the purpose statement. Complete this template before writing any informative message:

"As a result of this message, I want my audience to know _____."

Let's fill in some blanks:

- As a result of this message, I want my audience to know **how to make a successful sales call.**
- As a result of this message, I want my audience to know **how to order office supplies.**
- As a result of this message, I want my audience to know **how to operate the new computer.**

---

[1] Chapter 4 (Wake Partners) also addresses the informative message.

- As a result of this message, I want my audience to know **we're changing the way we award quarterly bonuses.**

Once you've filled in that important blank, you're ready to draft the message by starting with your launch.[2] To do so, you need to take context into account. What does your audience already know? Is the audience familiar with the situation or not? Is the audience expecting the information or not? Let's look at a particular situation, and let's say you want to write a memo to employees telling them we're changing the way we award quarterly bonuses. You're not persuading employees to accept the change—you've already made the change and you're simply announcing it. If we assume employees don't know the information is coming, you might launch your document this way:

> Because of our recent merger with EMCA, I'm writing to let you know we'll be changing the way we award bonuses next quarter. (I'd continue this message with the specifics of the why and the how.)

In this launch, I've taken context into account—the recent merger—as a way to provide a rationale for the information I'll be sharing. Now let's assume they've heard some rumblings through the grapevine about this issue. Here's how I might launch THIS variation:

> As you may know, we're changing the way we allocate quarterly bonuses. (As in the version above, I'd continue this message with specifics if I were going to complete it.)

Again, I had to take into account the context—the fact that some employees are already aware about this upcoming change. So when I say, "Consider what your audience knows about the situation," I want you to spend some time on this important step.

Once you've written a successful launch, you're ready to move into the substance of the document. Here's where you (1) add details, (2) clarify concepts, and/or (3) offer benefits. Whether you need all three elements, just two, or just one depends on your message. If we go back to the example informing employees we're changing the way we allocate quarterly bonuses, I would consider including:

- Details: I'd include information about when we start the new process and how we determine the amounts.

- Clarify concepts: If I have a number of new employees, I might briefly review the concept of "bonus allocation." However, if I don't have new employees, I won't need to clarify the concept of bonuses.

- Offer benefits: If I can see a benefit to employees—an increase in the percentage of bonuses—then I'd be sure to include that information.

Again, deciding whether to add details, clarify concepts, or offer benefits depends solely on the message and your audience. In terms of length, you may be able to complete this part of the message in one paragraph; however, if your information is complex, you may need additional paragraphs. That's fine. Just remember, be thorough in as few words as possible.

---

[2] If appropriate to the context and topic, you may find that you want to start with a friendly opening—a phrase or short sentence to lead into the launch.

After completing the details, you're ready to close. In general, keep the close positive as you link it to the topic and consider offering to answer questions:

> We all knew the merger would bring its own set of changes and challenges. So as we strive to keep our company competitive, I want to thank you for your hard work. If you have any questions about the change, please let me know.

To summarize, here's the outline you'll want to adapt to your informative message:

- **Launch** that takes "context" into account. If appropriate, you may preface the launch with a friendly opening.
- **Details, clarification(s), benefit(s).**
- **Positive close** linked to the topic.

That's about all you need to know to structure any informative message. Keeping this information in mind, I'd like you to read the following scenario and then draft an informative message.

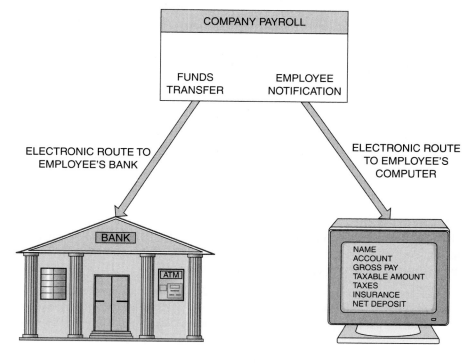

Paperless Paydays: Background

Today, more than 61 percent of U.S. wage earners receive their pay by direct deposit.[3] With direct deposit, employees don't get a paper check. They only get a paper stub, and their money goes directly into their bank accounts, saving them a trip to the bank. Now,

---

[3] National Automated Clearing House Association, http://www.nacha.org, accessed February 20, 2003.

some American companies are taking direct deposit a step further, offering paperless pay stubs. With this system, employees' checks are still deposited automatically; however, they access information about pay, deductions, benefits, and vacation/sick leave over the Internet or over the telephone. (See Exhibits 1 and 2 on pages 73–76.)

"Paperless paydays" can save big companies hundreds of thousands of dollars by eliminating printing and distribution costs. Microsoft Corp.(www.microsoft.com) estimates it saves $860,000 a year by using electronic payroll functions.[4] And American Greetings Corp. (www.americangreetings.com)—with more than 40,000 employees worldwide—saves an average of $20 per employee each year while also saving 92 hours each week in labor costs.[5]

While the benefits to companies are clear, employers considering paperless pay stubs need to anticipate and address employee concerns. For starters, companies need to be sure all employees can access the information—not all employees work at desks equipped with computers. In addition, companies need to assure *private* electronic access. Ingersoll-Rand Corporation (www.ingersoll-rand.com), a manufacturer of industrial and construction equipment with 30,000 U.S. employees and 120 facilities throughout the world, considered this issue when it adopted a paperless payroll system in late 2001. To address the challenge, the company installed computer and printer stations—designed much like voting booths to ensure privacy—throughout its production plants.

Employees also want assurances their employers take every possible precaution to protect personal salary information. According to a 2002 survey by the Federal Bureau of Investigation, computer hackers have attacked 90 percent of large U.S. corporations and government agencies.[6] And this threat doesn't just come from outside an organization. Many employees themselves have access to sensitive files stored on company computers, making personal information particularly vulnerable to inside jobs.

Understandably, then, employees will show varying degrees of acceptance toward paperless pay stubs. Research shows that just over half of employees are either "skeptical" of technological changes or "cling tightly" to current practices.[7] A Fortune 100 company that employs 6,500 people throughout the United States and Great Britain and produces software for various health care applications made the change to paperless pay stubs in 2003. According to the company's manager of Organization and People Development, employees weren't happy when they learned the company was abandoning paper stubs in favor of the paperless kind. This manager said:

> I believe we could have done a better job of communicating expectations around the change. We did not realize there were specific resources that we needed to help the process succeed. For example, printers weren't located in private areas for those employees who

---

[4] Samuel Greengard, "Pulp Fiction," http://www.businesstechnology.com/BT/Content/index.cfm/fuseaction/viewArticle/ContentID/63, accessed February 17, 2003.

[5] Jill Sherman, "Killer Intranet App Provides Fast ROI," http://www.intranetjournal.com/articles/200207/pit_07_12_02b.html, accessed February 17, 2003.

[6] 2002 survey by the Federal Bureau of Investigation.

[7] Tom Penderghast, "Easing Fear of New Technology. Nip Fear in the Bud" (1998), http://gbr.pepperdine.edu/983/change.html, accessed February 27, 2003.

needed to print their stubs at work. Looking back, I would have engaged members of the management team and employees in pre-conversion conversations so we could address their concerns early. I would have obtained information proactively rather than react to concerns as they occurred.

Without any sort of dialogue between employees and company executives, most employees resisted the transition.

American Greetings, on the other hand, mounted an aggressive internal communication campaign before adopting paperless pay stubs. Mark Hopton, director of Shared Services, said employees were cautious about the change at first because it represented a cultural shift for them. Just 25 years earlier, employees were paid in cash at the plants. Then, pay moved to paychecks and then to direct deposit. According to Hopton, "The question was 'how do we move beyond direct deposit?'" The company held meetings, put information on the company intranet, and sent letters to employees explaining the system and its benefits. To "sell" the change, Hopton said, "We over-communicated via every medium available to us." As a result, nearly everyone signed up for it.[8]

In addition to keeping communication channels open, companies also need to consider offering employees technical support via a call center, staffed to help employees negotiate the "sometimes" muddy waters of the online world.

Central Federal Bank and Paperless Stubs

Central Federal Bank (CFB) employs more than 100,000 people as analysts, auditors, branch managers, consultants, portfolio managers, tellers, cafeteria workers, and couriers. Located throughout the 48 contiguous United States, CFB offers the following services: ATMs; credit and debit cards; direct deposit; home mortgages; money market accounts; online banking; overdraft protection; personal and commercial checking accounts; personal, student, and vehicle loans; safe deposit boxes; and savings accounts.

Given CFB's size, location, and business model, the payroll department has considered the benefits of paperless pay stubs. According to Jim Canfield, director of ePayroll Business Development at TALX Corporation, "Companies no longer wonder IF they will go paperless with their pay stubs, they wonder WHEN."[9] After much research on the issues and discussion with corporate decision makers, the company has decided paperless stubs are a good idea.

Your Role

You're the company's vice president for Financial Administration.

Your Task

Discuss the best way to communicate your decision. According to American Greetings' Mark Hopton, "You need a clearly defined and developed plan which you can then

---

[8] Interview with Mark Hopton, September 1, 2004.

[9] Interview with Jim Canfield, September 11, 2004.

execute."[10] So formulate a communication strategy by answering the following questions:

1. What do you want to accomplish as a result of your message?

2. Identify the audience and its relationship to you. How will they likely react to your information?

3. Analyze your level of credibility with each of the audiences you identified. Will you need to build that credibility? If so, how?

4. What's the best communication medium/media for this situation? Considering possible employee concerns, what information should the communication include?

Deliverable

Once you believe you have a viable communication strategy, articulate that strategy in a memo to CFB's CEO. Then, assuming you get the green light, write an informative message to employees announcing the change. Be sure to follow the structure for an informative message, apply effective document design techniques,[11] and consider tone.[12]

---

[10] Interview with Mark Hopton, September 1, 2004.

[11] Chapter 4 (Wake Partners) addresses document design techniques in detail.

[12] Chapter 5 (It Has Come to My Attention) addresses tone within the context of employer/employee relationships.

Exhibit 1

Summary Electronic Statement

From focus groups, ePayroll learned that employees want an online summary statement. Employees also have the option of accessing payroll information via a phone interface. Jim Canfield, director of ePayroll Business Development for TALX Corporation, provided this telephone sample from Best Buy for you to try:

Best Buy: 1-866-802-3729

User ID: 825982598

Password: 82598

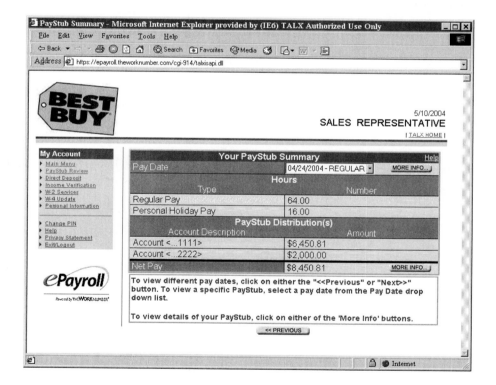

Source: Printed with permission from TALX.

Exhibit 2

Expanded Electronic Statement

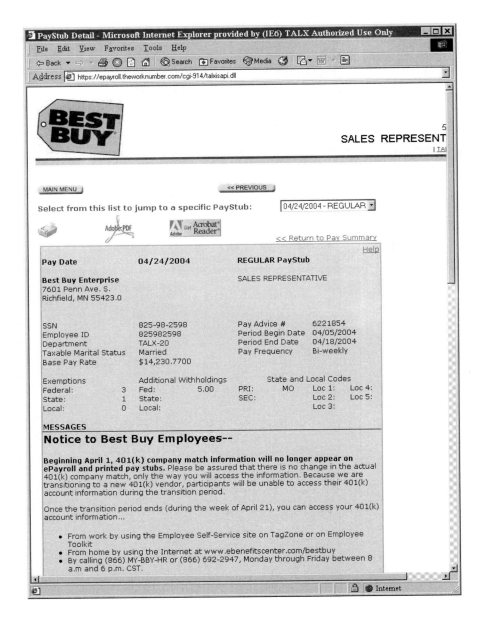

PayStub Detail - Microsoft Internet Explorer provided by (IE6) TALX Authorized Use Only

File   Edit   View   Favorites   Tools   Help

Back   Search   Favorites   Media

Address   https://epayroll.theworknumber.com/cgi-914/talxisapi.dll

BEST BUY

5
SALES REPRESENT

MAIN MENU   << PREVIOUS

Select from this list to jump to a specific PayStub: 04/24/2004 - REGULAR

Adobe PDF   Get Acrobat Reader   << Return to Pay Summary

Help

| Pay Date | 04/24/2004 | REGULAR PayStub |

Best Buy Enterprise   SALES REPRESENTATIVE
7601 Penn Ave. S.
Richfield, MN 55423.0

SSN	825-98-2598	Pay Advice #	6221854
Employee ID	825982598	Period Begin Date	04/05/2004
Department	TALX-20	Period End Date	04/18/2004
Taxable Marital Status	Married	Pay Frequency	Bi-weekly
Base Pay Rate	$14,230.7700		

Exemptions		Additional Withholdings		State and Local Codes		
Federal:	3	Fed:	5.00	PRI:	MO	Loc 1:	Loc 4:
State:	1	State:		SEC:		Loc 2:	Loc 5:
Local:	0	Local:				Loc 3:	

MESSAGES

Notice to Best Buy Employees--

Beginning April 1, 401(k) company match information will no longer appear on ePayroll and printed pay stubs. Please be assured that there is no change in the actual 401(k) company match, only the way you will access the information. Because we are transitioning to a new 401(k) vendor, participants will be unable to access their 401(k) account information during the transition period.

Once the transition period ends (during the week of April 21), you can access your 401(k) account information...

- From work by using the Employee Self-Service site on TagZone or on Employee Toolkit
- From home by using the Internet at www.ebenefitscenter.com/bestbuy
- By calling (866) MY-BBY-HR or (866) 692-2947, Monday through Friday between 8 a.m and 6 p.m. CST.

Internet

Exhibit 2

Expanded Electronic Statement (*continued*)

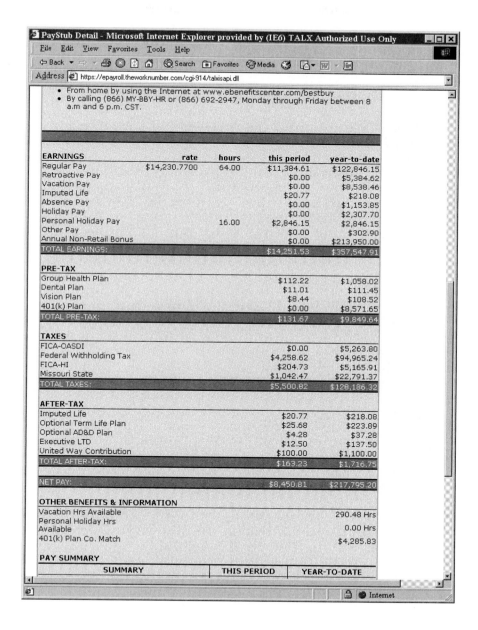

PayStub Detail - Microsoft Internet Explorer provided by (IE6) TALX Authorized Use Only

File Edit View Favorites Tools Help

Back | Search Favorites Media

Address https://epayroll.theworknumber.com/cgi-914/talxisapi.dll

- From home by using the Internet at www.ebenefitscenter.com/bestbuy
- By calling (866) MY-BBY-HR or (866) 692-2947, Monday through Friday between 8 a.m and 6 p.m. CST.

EARNINGS	rate	hours	this period	year-to-date
Regular Pay	$14,230.7700	64.00	$11,384.61	$122,846.15
Retroactive Pay			$0.00	$5,384.62
Vacation Pay			$0.00	$8,538.46
Imputed Life			$20.77	$218.08
Absence Pay			$0.00	$1,153.85
Holiday Pay			$0.00	$2,307.70
Personal Holiday Pay		16.00	$2,846.15	$2,846.15
Other Pay			$0.00	$302.90
Annual Non-Retail Bonus			$0.00	$213,950.00
TOTAL EARNINGS:			$14,251.53	$357,547.91

PRE-TAX		this period	year-to-date
Group Health Plan		$112.22	$1,058.02
Dental Plan		$11.01	$111.45
Vision Plan		$8.44	$108.52
401(k) Plan		$0.00	$8,571.65
TOTAL PRE-TAX:		$131.67	$9,849.64

TAXES		this period	year-to-date
FICA-OASDI		$0.00	$5,263.80
Federal Withholding Tax		$4,258.62	$94,965.24
FICA-HI		$204.73	$5,165.91
Missouri State		$1,042.47	$22,791.37
TOTAL TAXES:		$5,500.82	$128,186.32

AFTER-TAX		this period	year-to-date
Imputed Life		$20.77	$218.08
Optional Term Life Plan		$25.68	$223.89
Optional AD&D Plan		$4.28	$37.28
Executive LTD		$12.50	$137.50
United Way Contribution		$100.00	$1,100.00
TOTAL AFTER-TAX:		$163.23	$1,716.75

NET PAY:		$8,450.81	$217,795.20

OTHER BENEFITS & INFORMATION		
Vacation Hrs Available		290.48 Hrs
Personal Holiday Hrs Available		0.00 Hrs
401(k) Plan Co. Match		$4,285.83

PAY SUMMARY

SUMMARY	THIS PERIOD	YEAR-TO-DATE

Internet

Exhibit 2

Expanded Electronic Statement (*concluded*)

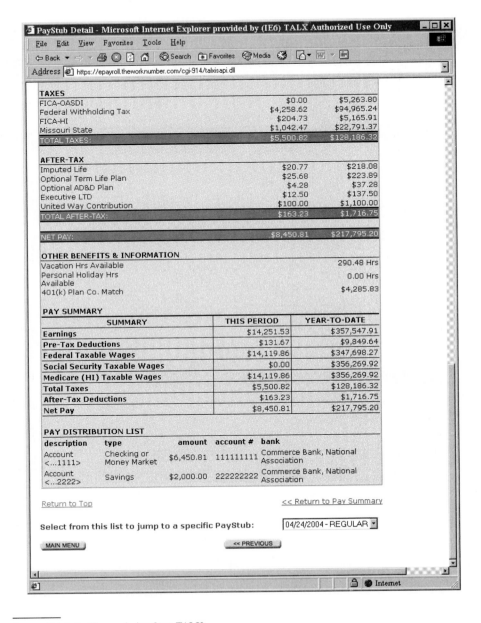

Source: Printed with permission from TALX.

7

Do Not Park Here . . . or Here . . . or Here

Chapter Emphasis

- **Structuring the Negative Message[1]**
- **Designing Effective Business Documents**
- **Adopting an Appropriate Business Tone**

Rationale

Bad news occurs on a continuum. News that announces cuts in jobs is much worse than news that announces cuts in cafeteria choices.

Bad News Continuum

Bad	Worse	Worst
Fewer cafeteria choices	No salary increases	Job cuts

So not all bad news is created equally. To make that point, this chapter immerses you in a context that's on the left side of the "bad news continuum." Later in the book, I'll immerse you in a scenario that's much more emotionally charged.

Chapter 5 contained the four elements that go into a negative message. Just in case you don't remember, let me remind you. They are:

1. Cushion
2. Bad news
3. Reasons for bad news; explanations; necessary details
4. Positive close

Let's briefly revisit each of these elements.

---

[1] See Chapter 5 (It Has Come to My Attention) for more information on organizing negative messages.

The Cushion

Which would you rather sit on? A or B?

A	B

When you need to communicate uncomfortable news to your audience (who may or may not know it's coming), you can soften the blow with an appropriate cushion. Take a look at the following cushions. Which are effective and why? Which are ineffective and why?

Telling an Applicant He Won't Be Getting the Job

1. Jason was by far the best-qualified candidate for the position.
2. Thank you for applying for the Brand Manager position with Fru-fru Shi-shi.
3. We're not offering you the job as Brand Manager.

Informing Employees They Won't Get Raises This Year

1. I know you worked your tail off this year.
2. You're not getting a raise.
3. This year, we had to make some tough economic choices.

Letting Employees Know You'll Be Temporarily Closing the Employee Lounge

1. We'll be closing the employee lounge on July 1.
2. I know you work hard every day, and I know how important it is to have a place where you can relax for a few minutes. In fact, when I get all stressed out, I like to close my office door, turn off the lights, and meditate.
3. So we can renovate the employee lounge, we'll be closing it on July 1.

The Bad News

The bad news is the "bottom line." It's your purpose for communicating. In general, you don't want to dwell on bad news. However, it should

- Come early in a message.
- Be direct, clear, and succinct.

Here are a few examples:

1. We won't be offering you a position at this time.

2. We're sorry but we can't open an account for you at this time.

3. Due to the current economic situation, we won't be able to give anyone a raise this year.

4. Effective July 1, we're closing the employee lounge.

Reasons/Explanations/Details

When you give your audience appropriate reasons, explanations, and details, you're helping your audience answer the question "why?"—why did I get this bad news? Look at these examples:

Example 1   In the following excerpt, the writer rejected a credit application based on information from a credit-reporting agency: That information answers the question "why?" for the reader . . . why didn't I get the credit card?

> While evaluating your application, *we received information from the credit-reporting agency named within this letter that affected our decision.*
>
> You may request a free copy of the agency's report if you do so no later than 90 days after you receive this letter. To do so, please contact their Consumer Relations Department directly. If you'd like to know the specific reasons for our decision, write us at the above address or contact us at 123-456-7890, Monday through Friday, 7:00 A.M.–7:00 P.M. EST.

Example 2   In this letter, the writer has refused to refund money to a hotel guest who didn't cancel a reservation. It answers the question "why?" . . . why didn't I get my refund?

> I have contacted OB, the hotel's General Manager. He told Guest Relations that the hotel is unable to issue credit because *reservations staff held a room available all night in anticipation of your arrival* the night of August 3. (Confirmation number 1234456.)

Example 3   In the following example, a bank has bumped a customer from Platinum status. Why? For not maintaining the right balance.

> To qualify for Platinum status, *you need to maintain a minimum daily balance of $100 in a checking account along with one of the following:*
>
> - Keep a regular savings account or money market account with a minimum daily balance of $1000, or

- Keep a $10,000 certificate of deposit, or
- Get a credit line of $15,000 or more.

Whether we agree with the news or disagree with the news, one thing needs to be clear: the reasons for the bad news. Our parents may have gotten away with "Because I said so," in response to "why? *why* can't I have a pet monkey?" But business communicators can't . . . they need to include specific reasons.

The Closing Paragraph

Once you've communicated the bad news and reasons, you're ready to close your message. Take a look at them and identify the ones you find effective:

1. In closing, we would like to assure you that we remain as committed as ever to helping you reach your financial goals. (To a brokerage customer)

2. We are delighted to have you as an AirMiles Member, and we look forward to seeing you onboard. (To a frequent flyer)

3. Thank you for your patience. We will strive to exceed your expectations for service in the future and look forward to serving you again soon. (To a credit card customer)

4. We look forward to seeing you at next week's meeting.

5. As we've done in the past, we'll continue to keep you informed. (To employees in the midst of company restructuring)

6. Above all, please remember that we are here to make electronic banking a simple but effective tool for you. We look forward to working with you and continuing to serve your financial needs. (To a banking customer)

7. Please contact me with any questions. (To an insurance customer)

8. We appreciate your interest in Mercedes-Benz Credit Corporation and wish you success in your future endeavors. (To a job applicant)

9. Thank you for everything you do every day for our clients and for each other.

10. We'll get back on track, or I'll make an example of somebody. (To employees from a frustrated manager)

Of the ones you identify as effective, what characteristic do they share? For me, the effective closings are positive, appreciative, professional, and short.

So let's see how you might apply the organizational strategy for a negative message in the next scenario.

DMP Pharmaceuticals and Parking Challenges

Headquartered in Boston, DMP Pharmaceuticals develops, manufactures, and markets prescription and over-the-counter medicines in its facilities throughout North America and Europe. More specifically, the company operates six research and development facilities and two consumer health facilities, and it employs 60,000 people.

Each facility operates as its own campus with multiple buildings and amenities. For example, most of the facilities include a cafeteria, library, wellness clinic, health club, shuttle services, and child care. And each facility also has the appropriate number of parking lots to accommodate its employees.

At the Pasadena, California, facility—which employs 2,000—the Division of Site Security maintains eight designated, clearly marked lots, described below:

1. **Employee parking.** Clearly marked signs direct employees to the appropriate parking areas within every lot.

2. **Handicapped parking.** Site Security has marked all handicapped parking clearly, which is a percentage of total parking spaces available. Because the law requires that parking lots set aside spaces for handicapped individuals, Site Security has the authority to ask law enforcement to cite offenders and to enforce towing of improperly parked vehicles.

3. **Visitor parking.** Site Security has allocated these spaces for those individuals who don't work for DMP's Pasadena facility. All visitors must sign in at one of the security desks and list their vehicle on a special vehicle log. DMP employees who park in these spaces receive a written warning from Site Security.

4. **Reserved parking.** Site Security has reserved a number of spaces for executive level employees. This "perk" helps maximize efficiency of the executives because they have to arrive and leave work sites multiple times within a given day.

5. **Specialty parking areas.** Several areas throughout the Pasadena campus have established parking for maintenance vehicles, safety vehicles, and facility shuttles. Employees (both handicapped and nonhandicapped), visitors, and executives are not allowed to park in these areas.

6. **Overflow area.** At times, all-staff events are held in the main auditorium in Building 3. When these events occur, employees may park along Scalybark Drive even though Site Security discourages it because that road is heavily traveled during most of the day. Site Security warns those who do decide to park there to use extreme caution when exiting and entering their vehicles.

7. **Circular drives.** Each building at the Pasadena facility is served by a wide, tree-lined circular drive that leads to each building entrance. These drives serve as areas for drop-off and pick-up of individuals and packages. As such, these areas are off-limits for parked vehicles.

8. **Waste disposal areas.** Site Security has posted signs asking employees not to block paths to the Dumpsters because having the waste company come back because a dumpster was blocked is costly to DMP.

In recent months, Site Security director Jeff Myers has noticed an increase in parking violations, so he's decided to institute a new plan for dealing with those employees who ignore the parking policy at DMP's Pasadena facility. He sat down with the Site Operating Committee and two of his officers to draft the plan. Proposed to Pasadena's executive team, the plan was wholeheartedly endorsed. For a

- **First Offense,** the employee receives a "Reminder Notice." This notice includes the specific violation, the vehicle description, the license number, the Site Security officer issuing the ticket, the date/time the ticket was issued, and the specific lot.

- **Second Offense,** the employee receives a "Reminder Ticket," and the employee's supervisor gets a note. The "Reminder Ticket" is identical to the "Reminder Notice" except for its name.
- **Third Offense,** the employee receives a "Level 1 Ticket," and the employee's supervisor and HR get notes. The supervisor provides an "occurrence note" to HR for the employee's file.
- **Fourth Offense,** the employee receives a "Level 2 Ticket," and the employee's supervisor and HR get notes. The supervisor provides a "written reprimand," which goes to HR for the employee's file.
- **Fifth Offense,** the employee receives a "Final Ticket," and the supervisor terminates the employee.

In addition to these measures, Site Security has the authority to cite and tow any vehicle parked in an unauthorized place. Once an employee gets a ticket, a one-year enforcement period kicks in. If the employee doesn't receive another ticket within that one-year period, Site Security will then wipe that employee's record clean.

Your Role

You are employed at DMP's Pasadena facility in the Site Security office.

Your Task

Jeff Myers has asked you to write a message to all DMP Pasadena employees reminding them of the current parking regulations and informing them of the new plan for dealing with violators.

Additional Task

Design the "Reminder Notice" for the first offense that Site Security officers can place on car windshields.

Your Audience

All employees at the Pasadena facility.

Nuts and Bolts

- Decide on and clarify your purpose. You're "laying down the law," so the message is negative. Do you want to include a rationale for the message?
- As you consider audience, what tone do you want to adopt?
- Given the structure of the Pasadena facility, what's the best communication channel? Can you think of multiple possible communication channels?
- Be sure to follow an appropriate organizational strategy for a negative message.
- Consider options for effective layout.
- Limit your message to one page.

8

Special "No Interest/No Payments for 12 Months" Promotion

Chapter Emphasis

* **Structuring the Persuasive Message**
* **Analyzing Your Audience, Choosing the Right Information, and "Distilling and Clumping" That Information**

Rationale

Often in your career, you'll need to ask your co-workers and customers to act—to do something. For example, you might want your co-workers to approve a new marketing plan, your executive team to allocate a big budget for your research project, or your customers to order several thousand cases of your new product. To be successful, then, you need strong persuasive skills, and this chapter gives you the opportunity to practice those skills.

The Persuasive Framework

Consider including the following elements when you're trying to persuade your audience:

* **Bottom line:** You'll need to include a bottom line that clearly articulates what you want your audience *to do*. The key phrase here is "to do" because you want your audience to act. In a persuasive message, the "bottom line" implicitly recognizes we have a problem we need to solve or an opportunity we want to explore.

* **Details:** People are curious creatures by nature, and that curiosity often manifests itself in questions. Within the context of a persuasive message, you'll be more successful if you anticipate and answer those questions. In doing so, you're providing the necessary details a reader needs in order to act. All of us like to think of ourselves as rational beings who can be persuaded to act with enough of

the right concrete, relevant information. So anticipate the questions your audience could raise within the context of your topic and answer them. The most important question to anticipate is **"why?"** Why are you asking me to act? Why should I act? Your answers to this question provide the rationale for your bottom line and the benefits to your audience. You should also consider additional questions that include **How? When? Where? Who?**

Let me make one more point about the **details.** Earlier in this book, I said people like to think of themselves as rational. They want to believe they make decisions based on the facts—on hard evidence. And that's true . . . in part. However, people are also human, which means they're susceptible to a wide range of emotions. Marketers have long recognized this fact. Given this characteristic, I'd like to urge you to incorporate relevant stories into your persuasive messages when appropriate. I've heard it said that successful persuasion is only 50 percent logic and facts and 50 percent emotion. Indeed, emotional arguments can be powerfully persuasive when coupled with "the facts." (See Chapter 2, page 34 for a more in-depth look at how to incorporate stories into business messages.)

- **Action Steps:** Give your audience instructions for what you expect them to do next.

As always, adapt this framework to your persuasive messages, but feel free to "tweak" it for your specific purpose.

Distilling and Clumping Information

Choosing the right details, information, and support is one of the hardest jobs in drafting any message. However, once you've gathered the data, you have to package that data in a way that's digestible for your audience. That is, you need to clump information because "rhetorical clumps" are easier to digest than are bunches of unrelated information. For example, I wouldn't mix information from the "fiscal year 2005 forecast" with those from the "fiscal year 2004 results." I probably wouldn't mix details for "improving our operation" with the details related to "integrating our new acquisitions." You need to create categories from your information because doing so will help you structure the details.

The following business scenario gives you the opportunity to practice framing a persuasive argument while distilling and clumping information.

Background

The Appliance Center—which has more than 750 stores throughout the United States—sells products for the kitchen and laundry room, including refrigerators, ranges, disposals, gas grills, microwaves, stoves, washers, and dryers. And customers are usually happy to learn the company stocks all the major brands on location at its stores.[1]

---

[1] The company carries Amana, Asko, Bosch, Broan, Frigidaire, GE, Hotpoint, Jenn-Air, KitchenAid, Magic Chef, Maytag, Sharp, Thermidor, and Whirlpool. It can also order specialty brands.

To boost sales for the coming quarter, the company's leading credit managers developed a promotion to offer customers a special "No Interest/No Payments for 12 Months" promotion. Having communicated the plan and received "buy-in" from the company's store managers and operations managers, the Appliance Center's Credit Division must now communicate information about the promotion to the company's more than 44,000 employees. Look at this "list of specifics," decide which overarching categories emerge, and write those down. You may then decide to use those categories to create headings for your message. Also, given the audience, decide what information is and is not essential.

- Your instructor will provide you with the dates for the "No Interest/No Payments for 12 Months" promotion.
- Customers must have an active Appliance Center Consumer Credit Card to qualify for this promotion.
- The promotion is only good on purchases of $199 or more that customers make on their Appliance Center Consumer Credit Card.
- The purchase must be on a single receipt.
- Some customers will have bought credit insurance.
- Credit insurance pays for the balance on a credit card in case the cardholder can't make payments.
- Credit insurance is optional.
- Customers have to present a coupon to the cashier when they're ready to pay for their purchase.
- Employees need to have coupons available for customers.
- Employees should keep coupons in their shirt pockets.
- Employees need to be sure coupon bins and bulletin boards remain well stocked.
- Employees should return coupons to customers after scanning coupons.
- Customers can learn about the promotion through in-store signs, television, radio, and newspaper advertisements.

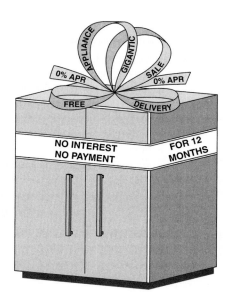

- The Credit Division will assess finance charges and credit insurance charges on the promotional purchases and add those charges to the account each month during the promotion period.
- No payments on finance charges or optional credit insurance charges are due until the promotion period ends.

- If customers make full payment of the promotional purchase and any optional insurance charges before the end of the promotional period, the Credit Division will reverse all finance charges assessed during the 12-month period.

- For previously existing balances and nonpromotional purchases, the Credit Division will assess finance charges and optional insurance charges each month.

- The Credit Division will require customers to pay the minimum amount on previously existing balances and nonpromotional purchases as usual.

- For more information, employees need to contact their store manager, operations manager, district operations manager, or the manager on duty at the Appliance Center Credit Division (1-877-123-4567).

- Front-end cashiers should always remember to ask customers if they want this purchase on their Appliance Center credit card.

- Employees should encourage those customers without a card to apply for the card through the Appliance Center's Credit Division. The process for applying for an Appliance Center consumer credit card is quick.

- If a customer asks, What purchases qualify for the special "No Interest/No Payments for 12 Months" promotion, employees should answer the following: When a customer presents the coupon, every purchase made on the Appliance Center's Consumer Credit Card of $199 or more during the promotional period qualifies for special "No Interest/No Payments for 12 Months" promotion.

- If a customer asks, Do business accounts qualify for this offer?, employees should answer the following: No.

- If a customer asks, When does the promotion end, employees should answer the following: (NOTE: Your instructor will provide you with this information.)

- If a customer asks, When will my purchase appear on my bill?, employees should answer the following: Customer purchases with this promotion will appear on the next monthly statement.

- The Appliance Center Credit Division will still bill customers for their optional credit insurance.

- Optional credit insurance charges on nonpromotion purchases will be due monthly.

- Optional credit insurance charge on promotion purchases will be due anytime before the end of the 12-month period.

- If a customer asks, Will interest be on my bill?, employees should answer the following: Yes, customers will see interest added to their balances each month. However, if customers pay the purchase amount and any optional insurance charges in full by the promotional expiration date—indicated on the bill—the Credit Division will reverse all accrued interest.

- If a customer asks, What will happen to my nonpromotional balance?, employees should answer the following: Customers will need to make regular payments on the nonpromotional balance but not on the new promotional purchases.

- If a customer asks, May I make payments each month until paid?, employees should answer the following: Yes, customers may make payments at any time and for any amount.

- If a customer asks, If I spend $50 one day, and $150 the next day for a total of $200, does that qualify for the Special "No Interest/No Payments for 12 Months" promotion?, employees should answer the following: No, each receipt must equal $199 or more to qualify for the promotion.

- If a customer asks, If my purchases total $200, then I return an item for $100, will I get the "No Interest/No Payments for 12 Months" promotion?, employees should answer the following: Yes, since the original purchase was $199 or more.

- If a customer asks, What will the minimum payment be each month when the first payment is due?, employees should answer the following: Customers will need to pay the minimum payment of $20 when the first payment is due.

- If a customer asks, For the "No Interest/No Payments for 12 Months" promotion, do I have to pay off the entire balance within 12 months for purchases through this promotion?, employees should answer the following: No. However, if customers wish to avoid paying finance charge on the promotional purchases, they'll need to pay the promotional balance and any optional insurance charges in full within 12 months.

- Regular credit terms apply to nonpromotional purchases.

- APR is 18 percent.

- APR is 11.1 percent for purchases of $2,000 or more.

- The minimum finance charge per month is $1.00.

- This promotion is subject to credit approval.

- This promotion excludes business accounts.

Your Role

After graduating from college three years ago, you joined the Appliance Center's management team at its headquarters in San Diego. Today, you're one of several assistants in the Consumer Credit Division. Your superior, VP of the Consumer Credit Division, has asked you to convey information about this promotion to store employees and to customers.

Your Tasks

Draft a message to store employees communicating the highlights of the promotion.

Draft a message (flyer, newspaper insert, or form letter), targeting potential customers and persuading them to take advantage of the promotional campaign. Design the promotion coupon. Be sure to complete a communication strategy before drafting your message.

CHAPTER 9

Fewer Injuries for Warehouse Employees

Chapter Emphasis

- **Structuring the Persuasive Message**
- **Communicating with Employees**
- **Designing Effective Documents**
- **Crafting an Effective Persuasive Presentation**
- **Doing Primary and Secondary Research**

Rationale

See Chapter 8, "No Interest/No Payments," for rationale.

Background

People who work in large retail warehouses—stores like Costco, Home Depot, Lowe's Home Improvement Warehouse, and Wal-Mart—spend much of their time moving and lifting large, heavy merchandise. Craig, who works at a Lowe's Home Improvement Warehouse, is all too aware of the strength required to do his job: "Things can get pretty heavy. I mean, when you pick up a generator, it's an armload. And a bag of cement over there near lumber can weigh 80 or 90 pounds."[1]

As a result, many employees like Craig suffer from on-the-job injuries, and the numbers are staggering. "The total cost of disabling workplace injuries is up to $42.5 billion"[2] from $20 billion just over 10 years ago.[3] The Bureau of Labor Statistics recorded more than 5 million on-the-job injuries and illnesses in 2001, which resulted in

---

[1] Interview, Lowe's Store, Durham, North Carolina, June 24, 2003.

[2] Caroline McDonald, *Injury Costs Skyrocket, Study Finds* (May 12, 2003). National Underwriter. Retrieved June 1, 2003, from http://proquest.umi.com/.

[3] Don B. Chaffin, and Lawarence J. Fine, ed. *A National Strategy for Occupational Musculoskeletal Injuries—Implementation Issues and Research Needs* (November 1992), U.S. Department of Health and Human Services. Public Health Services. Centers for Disease Control and Prevention. National Institute for Occupational Safety and Health.

more than 1.5 million days away from work.[4] Most of those injuries—28 percent—were back-related and resulted from "overexertion from manually lifting, pushing, pulling, and carrying goods."[5]

Lowe's, where Craig works, is aware of this problem and seeks to keep its employees safe and healthy. "They [management] make us wear these back belts. We're supposed to fasten them when we're lifting something heavy and loosen them when we're not. But I always keep my belt attached just so I don't forget."[6]

As the second largest retailer in the United States, Home Depot also takes seriously the safety of its more than 300,000 employees.[7] The company not only strives to operate within stringent safety guidelines but also seeks to ensure that its associates understand the connection between being in shape and reduced on-the-job injuries. Each of the 1,500 warehouses has its own wellness representative.[8] And since 1987, Home Depot has promoted its "Building Better Health" (BBH) Program. Targeted to the company's employees, the BBH program offers resources that address nutrition and physical fitness.[9] These resources include fitness-related brochures, which cover stretching, exercising, and lifting. "The Importance of Stretching" brochure provides the rationale and benefits of stretching as well as information on how to stretch correctly. In addition to advocating for "stretch break[s]" at work, the brochure includes a 10-minute stretch routine.[10]

"Exercising for Better Health," another brochure, includes information about the benefits of exercise. It also includes the following steps for starting a successful exercise program:

1.   Set attainable goals.

2.   Find a partner.

---

[4] *Injuries, Illnesses, and Fatalities. Latest Numbers* (2001). Retrieved from http://www.bls.gov/iif/home.htm#tables.

[5] Caroline McDonald, *Injury Costs Skyrocket, Study Finds* (May 12, 2003). National Underwriter. Retrieved June 1, 2003, from http://proquest.umi.com/.

[6] Interview, Lowe's Store, Durham, North Carolina, June 24, 2003. NOTE: Health experts don't agree on the effectiveness of the belt. However, many retail establishments require their employees to wear the belts.

[7] Home Depot operates more than 1,500 stores across North America and China. Each warehouse stocks more than 35,000 kinds of building, home improvement, and lawn and garden supplies. And to help customers turn all those supplies into finished projects, Home Depot offers "how-to" clinics that teach customers how to lay ceramic tile, install an irrigation system, or build a backyard deck. Home Depot also offers "design and decorating consultations, truck and tool rental, home delivery, [and] free [plant] potting. . . ." Corporate overview (n.d.), retrieved June 17, 2003, from http://www.homedepot.com/HDUS/EM_US/corporate/about/corp_overview.shtml.

[8] *The Home Depot Social Responsibility Report* (2000). Retrieved July 9, 2003, from http://www.homedepot.com/HDUS/EN_US/compinfo/community/social_responsibility/2000/healthsafe.html.

[9] *Home Depot Benefits Info* (n.d.). Retrieved June 19, 2003, from http://www.recruitingsite.com/corpfiles/homedepot/benefits.htm.

[10] *The Importance of Stretching* (n.d.). From Home Depot's Building Better Health Program. Publication Number HDM-052.

3. Start slowly.

4. Have fun![11]

The "Back Health" brochure indicates "[w]orking at Home Depot is a very physical occupation and injuries are bound to occur. But that doesn't mean we should forget about doing things the right way." To that end, this brochure includes some revealing statistics from the company's "Risk Management Report," which I've included here:

*   Most often injured body part: the lower back.

*   Most often nature of injury: sprains and strains.

*   Most often cause of injury: improper lifting.

*   Most often activity when injured: lifting object.

*   Most often injured departments: front end, outside garden, lumber.

*   Most often type of injury: overexertion.

As a way to help employees avoid these kinds of injuries, the "Back Health" brochure also includes (1) information about aerobic, strength, and flexibility training, (2) instructions for wearing the "Back Support Belt" properly, (3) tips for lifting heavy or awkward objects properly, and (4) lifting techniques with names such as the "Forklift," the "Golfer's Lift," and the "Knee Lift."[12] Indeed, the "Building Better Health Program" seeks to protect the health of Home Depot employees.

Can lead to back problems
and injuries = Loss of Productivity

Can avoid back problems
and injuries = Increase in Productivity

The Scenario

Like Lowes and The Home Depot, Big Kit Warehouse (BKW) runs a chain of working retail warehouses. Headquartered in a major metropolitan area in southwestern United States, BKW operates 169 stores and employs around 680 people. The company sells a

---

[11] *Exercising for Better Health* (n.d.). From Home Depot's Building Better Health Program. Publication Number HDM-055.

[12] *Back Health* (n.d.). From Home Depot's Building Better Health Program. Publication Number HDM-051.

variety of merchandise for home improvement "do-it-yourselfers." Given the physical exertion employees experience on a daily basis, BKW has decided to develop and introduce its own "Health and Wellness Program."

First, the company plans to develop and distribute leaflets that educate employees on various health-related topics. Next, the company plans to develop and offer quarterly "wellness events" for employees at each of its stores. As part of the "wellness events," BKW fitness staff will offer a two-stage incentive program to those employees who sign up for one or more of the following online health clinics:

- "Breathe Your Way to Better Health," designed to help employees quit smoking.
- "Eat Your Way to Better Health," designed to help employees lose weight.
- "Exercise Your Way to Better Health," designed to help employees get in shape.
- "Sleep Your Way to Better Health," designed to help employees increase alertness during the day.
- "Manage Your Way to Better Health," designed to help employees manage their time both at work and at home.

Those employees who complete these one-hour online clinics receive a T-shirt and smock pin. These employees are then eligible to move to stage two of the incentive program. In this stage, the company offers paid leave to employees for "pounds off," "smokeless days," and "improved body mass index." For example, those employees who lose 10 percent of their body weight, remain smoke free for six months, or improve their body mass index by 10 percent receive three days of paid leave.

Your Role

You work as a "Benefits Specialist" in the Benefits Division within the Department of Human Resources. You're located at BKW's corporate headquarters.

Your Audience

Employees at BKW. How would you characterize them? Busy? Lots of time to read? Access to email? They probably have two 15-minute breaks in a typical eight-hour shift.

Your Task

Elaine Tipiliac, VP of Human Resources, has asked you to write a companywide message introducing employees to the new program and persuading them to (1) pick up and read the new leaflets once the stores receive them; (2) participate in the quarterly wellness events; and (3) sign up for the online health clinics.

Additional Task

Design one or more of the following leaflets:

- Stretching techniques
- Nutrition

- Hydration
- Smoking cessation techniques
- Sleep

To design each leaflet, consider following these steps: choose one of the topics and complete primary and secondary research by (1) interviewing experts in the field and (2) reading professional articles. Then provide a

1. Rationale for the topic—why should employees be concerned about it?
2. Benefits of the topic—what explicit and implicit benefits will employees experience?
3. Relevant statistics for the topic.
4. How-to information for the topic.
5. Any additional information you deem appropriate to the topic.

Once you've gathered the appropriate information, design the document using appropriate document design techniques. (See Chapter 1, "Business Writing Basics," pp. 26–30 and Chapter 4, "Wake Partners," pp. 53–59 for an in-depth discussion of document design.)

Additional Task

Develop talking points for the wellness events persuading employees to sign up for one or more online health clinics. Supplement your talk with information about the two-stage incentive program. Consider supplementing the talking points with appropriate PowerPoint slides. (See Chapter 2, "Business Speaking Basics," for information on structuring a presentation.)

10

Midwest University Named Number One Party School

Chapter Emphasis

- **Researching and Writing Proposals**
- **Designing Documents**

Rationale

While most writers propose ideas on 8½ × 11 paper, when Herb Kelleher and a partner conceived of the idea that would become Southwest Airlines, they did so on a cocktail napkin. Indeed, in the world of work, things change because people have ideas they've proposed in writing. Because proposal writing is such an important skill, I've included the scenario in this chapter to give you some practice. However, before you begin writing, you'll want to review pages 26–30, "Document Design Matters" in Chapter 1, pages 32–35, "Supporting General Claims" in Chapter 2, and pages 53–59 in Chapter 4.

Generating Content

As you go about generating the content for a proposal, you need to anticipate the questions your proposal will raise in your audience's mind. To demonstrate this point to my students, I told them I wanted to propose an automobile engine cooker. The concept was simple—buy frozen dinner ingredients from the grocery store on your way home from work, place them in the compartmentalized container mounted on top of your car's engine, drive home, and serve the steaming food.

I got a few strange stares from my students, so I asked them what questions this concept raised in their minds. Here are some of those questions:

- How much will it cost?
- What competition exists? Is anybody doing this?

- Are there any health risks? How dangerous is it to use?
- What's the target market?
- Will you market it to the auto industry or a specific manufacturer?
- What will it look like?
- What are the barriers to entering this market?
- Why would anyone want to buy it?

The exercise was useful because it showed me (and my students!) the kinds of questions an idea raises. So when you're writing a proposal or pitching an idea, pose the idea to a mock audience and ask them what questions the concept raises. If your mock audience has questions, your real audience will as well. Use the answers to generate your content.

Plugging Content into a Framework

In general, you'll follow this broad framework when you write a proposal. Just be sure to fine-tune it to your purpose:

- Introduction with appropriate background material and bottom line
- Problem, opportunity, idea
- Solution, implementation, recommendation

Proposal Elements

When you're out in the work world, you'll probably discover your organization has its own requirements about what a proposal should contain and how it should look. So I don't want to be prescriptive and say, "Here's what your proposal must include." Instead, I'd prefer to give you some guidelines about what a proposal can include:

Transmittal Message   This document says to the reader what you'd say to the reader if you were handing the report over in person. In essence, it says, "Here's my proposal." You're welcome to include the key findings, highlights, and the recommendation. But again, this document does what its name says it does: it transmits.

Cover/Title Page   Include the title, your name, the recipient's name, and the date. Balance the information on the page so it looks good to your eyeballs.

Table of Contents and List of Figures   If your document is somewhat long, you should help your audience find information easily. To that end, you may include a table of contents and list of figures with page numbers.

Executive Summary   If you have a long document or a boss with attention deficit disorder, consider including an executive summary. It's a mini version of the longer document. And it contains enough relevant information so a busy executive has information to make an informed decision based on your recommendation.

Body   You have to include this part. It's the meat, the main course, the featured attraction . . . you get the idea.

Appendices   Integrating visuals within text helps minimize the "back-and-forth flip." However, when you have visuals that take up a page, you should consider putting them in an appendix. Just be sure you refer your audience to the appendix, you number each, title each, and tell your audience the significance of each.

The Scenario

Midwest University (MU) lies in the heart of the country's Corn Belt. This flagship university enrolls more than 30,000 students, offers more than 300 degree programs at the undergraduate and graduate levels, and boasts 32 NCAA titles among its various varsity athletic teams. Major news outlets have recognized the university as tops in the country for its academic rigor, its culture, and its beauty.

Last year—just before the start of the new school year—MU received another top ranking—*The College and University Review* named MU as the country's #1 party school. Seeing the ranking as irresponsible because it gives students a distorted notion of what it means to party on a college campus, the American Medical Association characterized the "party school" ranking as irresponsible. And while university administrators weren't too happy with the ranking, MU student Janie Adams commented, "The bar scene at MU offers students the chance to socialize—hang out with friends, wind down after a day of classes. . . . So I think the ranking is great."

This kind of attitude has universities concerned because alcohol use continues to be widespread at many U.S. institutions of higher learning. In a recent study from more than 55,000 students on 132 college and university campuses, more than 72 percent of college students said they had used alcohol at least once during the past 30 days; more than 84 percent said they had used alcohol at least once during the past year.[1]

These percentages, however, don't tell the whole "alcohol" story for college students. A significant number of students report either missing class or falling behind in school work because of alcohol consumption.[2] And alcohol consumption on campus has produced even more sobering statistics. Each year more than

- 600,000 students are victims of assault by another student who has been drinking,
- 70,000 students are victims of alcohol-related sexual assault,
- 500,000 students are unintentionally injured under the influence of alcohol, and
- 1,400 college students die each year from alcohol-related unintentional injuries.[3]

One mother whose college-aged child died in an alcohol-related incident said, "[I]f someone had told me that every year or so someone dies on campus, I would have had to think twice before I sent my [child] there."[4]

At MU, Luke Lawrence, an 18-year-old business major, died November 13, 2000, after suffocating on his own vomit. The coroner determined he had elevated alcohol levels in his blood. Just over two years later—on February 22, 2003—Alex Vanderburgh, a 20-year-old biology major, died. He suffered a fatal skull fracture when he hit his head on a cement patio after performing a keg stand.

Because the university has reminded students at the start of each academic year about the risks of drinking alcohol, MU officials were understandably upset with the

---

[1] Results from the 2000 study conducted by The Core Institute at Southern Illinois University. http://www.siu.edu/departments/coreinst/public_html/recent.html. Date of access: May 18, 2003.

[2] Amy M. Wolaver, "Effects of Heavy Drinking in College on Study Effort, Grade Point Average, and Major Choice," *Contemporary Economic Policy* 20, no. 4 (October 2002), pp. 415–28. Note also: This study tied college drinking to reduced earnings among both college-educated men and women. See also Henry Wechsler, George W. Dowdall, Andrea Davenport, and William DeJong, "Binge Drinking on Campus: Results of a National Study." Higher Education Center. http://www.edu.org/hec/pubs/binge.htm. Date of access: June 3, 2003.

[3] R. Hingson, T. Heeren, R. Zakocs, A. Kopstein, and H. Wechsler, "Magnitude of Alcohol-Related Morbidity, Mortality, and Alcohol Dependence among U.S. College Students Age 18–24," *Journal of Studies on Alcohol* 63, no. 2 (2002), pp. 136–44. See also Mark Clayton, "Fuller Picture Emerges of College Drinking. For the First Time, a Study Tallies Number of Alcohol-Related Deaths Nationwide," *Christian Science Monitor,* September 29, 1999, p. 2.

[4] Clayton, "Fuller Picture Emerges," p. 2.

"party school" ranking. The ranking undermined the university's philosophy, and it garnered unwanted attention in the mainstream press. The ranking also attracted additional interest when the "wild girls" television crew rolled into town and spent several days at local bars filming the university's co-eds.

To voice his displeasure with the ranking, Hubert Harrison, the university's president, telephoned *The College and University Review*'s editor-in-chief, Jeffrey Benton. In his conversation, Harrison characterized the ranking as careless and unscientific. In response, Benton said he'd continue to include the ranking because students always comment on the social scene at their universities.

Shortly after that conversation, President Harrison wrote his annual letter reminding students about MU's alcohol policies, which was published in *The Midwest Voice,* the school's student newspaper. (See Exhibit 1 for a copy of the letter.) However, knowing he needed to do more, he scheduled a meeting with several university officials to address in more detail the problem of drinking on campus. At that meeting, he listed steps a number of other universities had already taken:

- One institution now includes a detailed, graphic three-hour session during orientation that shows incoming students the darker side of alcohol abuse.

- At that same institution, all resident advisors (RAs) have to participate in a special "Alcohol Awareness" seminar before the start of each academic year with a refresher course before the second semester. This program teaches RAs how to recognize the signs of alcohol abuse, how to counsel affected students, and how to respond to alcohol-related emergencies. Moreover, this university exercises its right to notify parents if their underage child has been caught drinking.[5]

- To ensure ongoing discussions about the problems of alcohol, a liberal arts college created the Student Alcohol Awareness Advisory Board (SAAAB) to bring a student perspective to the college's alcohol policies.

- A top-tier university adjusted its curriculum in an effort to impact the traditional Thursday-night party scene. For the first time in 12 years, that university substantially increased the number of required core classes held on Friday mornings.

- At the same top-tier university, the Center on Alcohol Abuse and Prevention offers training to the town's bartenders on how to recognize the signs of intoxication and how to respond to alcohol emergencies. The culture on campus has also changed, and university police have cracked down on alcohol-related arrests, which have increased fivefold.

After talking about these measures with those at the meeting and addressing how MU might respond to its own situation, President Harrison created the Alcohol Awareness Task Force made up of students. President Harrison asked them to research, develop, and propose solutions that address the drinking culture at MU.

---

[5] S. Burd, "Colleges Allowed to Tell Parents About Alcohol Abuse," *Chronicle of Higher Education,* July 14, 2000, p. A31.

Exhibit 1

Letter from MU President Hubert Harrison Published in *The Midwest Voice*

President Harrison wrote this letter to MU students after his conversation with the editor-in-chief of *The College and University Review*.

LEARNING, INTEGRITY, and HONOR

**OFFICE OF THE PRESIDENT
MIDWEST UNIVERSITY
FOUNDED 1893**

Dear Students:

Welcome to the start of a brand new academic year. With the excitement of moving into the dorms, arranging your course schedule, and meeting new friends, I'd like to take this opportunity to remind you of MU's Alcohol Policy.

Any person under 21 years of age is prohibited from possessing or using alcoholic beverages both on and off campus. Any person who violates this policy will be formally charged by the university and will participate in a hearing. If convicted, said person may experience one or more of the following sanctions: lose academic credit and/or financial aid, be suspended or expelled, go for required evaluations and treatment, perform community service, and/or be assigned to serve on the Student Alcohol Awareness Advisory Board (SAAAB). Finally, the laws of our state will be enforced.

Keep in mind, if you live on campus, your RA is an invaluable resource who can help you address many alcohol-related concerns. In addition, you can call Student Psychological Services—a division of MU's student health—at 7-3456 for guidance.

Have a wonderful semester and academic year.

Sincerely,

President H. Harrison

President Hubert Harrison

Your Role

You're a student at MU, and President Harrison has appointed you to the Alcohol Awareness Task Force.

Your Task

Together with the committee, draft a proposal to President Harrison detailing your ideas for dealing with alcohol on the MU campus.

Your Audience

Target your proposal to President Harrison and his vice presidents. Exhibit 2 details the university's organizational structure and shows where President Harrison fits within that framework. Using the communication strategy framework on Chapter 3, consider the kinds of issues (related to alcohol consumption) that are important to each VP.

Exhibit 2

Midwest University's Organizational Chart

Each division is headed by a vice president.

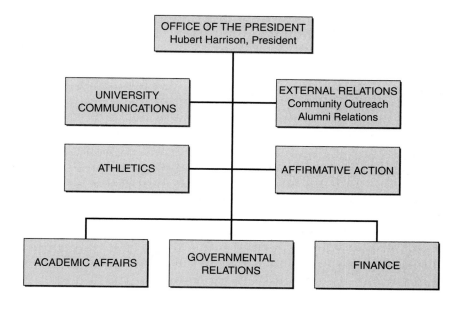

Nuts and Bolts

- Decide on and clarify your purpose. Is it to lobby for a "marketing campaign," a course, new policies, a combination of these approaches, or something else? Is it to inform students about the university's stance on alcohol policies? Is it something else?

- While this scenario provides a few examples of how colleges and universities are responding to on-campus drinking, you'll want to strengthen your proposal with additional research.

- Follow an appropriate organizational strategy and include an appropriate style and tone.

- Consider options for an effective layout. Be sure to incorporate visuals.

- Be sure the document is grammatically and mechanically correct.

11

The Big National Presentation

Chapter Emphasis

- **Developing and Delivering a Presentation**
- **Doing Research**

Rationale

In the business arena, when you get up to give a presentation, people notice you. However, most of us don't like that kind of attention. That's because so much is at stake—but THAT's precisely the reason TO present—when a lot's at stake, you've got a lot to gain. Besides, what's the worse thing that could happen?[1]

The question is then: How do you reconcile this preference for not speaking in public with this business and professional need to promote your ideas and—by extension—yourself? The answer lies in approaching the task systematically. First, always start by asking this important question: What do I want my audience to do or to know as a result of hearing my presentation? Please go back and re-read that sentence. It's an important sentence. With your purpose clearly articulated, you're ready to gather content and plug it into a framework. Next, you need to develop the appropriate accompanying material—slides, handouts, and supplements. Finally, you need to practice your delivery skills so you convey your content with confidence.

You may want to refresh your memory on these important concepts by taking another look at Chapter 2, "Business Speaking Basics." It addresses all of these topics in detail. Once you do so, you'll be prepared to tackle this business scenario.

---

[1] I used to have the luxury of asking, "What's the worst that could happen?" Here's the worst thing: In February 2004, Dennis Pelletier, executive director for a New York water authority, was speaking to a group of 600 people when he fell backward from the podium and died. My goodness. (J.M. Odato and Kate Gurnett, "Executive Dies during County's Conference," *The Times Union*, February 3, 2004.)

Scenario

When she graduated from college in 1989 with a degree in urban planning, Myrtle Hart started working for her father's commercial building business. Then in 1994, she started her own company. During the last 10 years, she's designed and developed three mixed-use communities that balance residential areas with commercial areas and open spaces.

Her most recent project—TerraMont, located outside Atlanta, Georgia—just received national attention earlier this year when The National Alliance for Environmental Concerns awarded it the "Silver Medal for Urban Sensitivity." In conjunction with the award, Myrtle won a contract to construct an "Earth House" at TerraMont. In keeping with the spirit of the award, the "Earth House" will use only environmentally sensitive materials, conform to the natural topography of the earth, and preserve as much of the natural landscape as possible. Once completed, the house will appear on the cover of the widely sold *Hearth and Garden* magazine. In addition, the magazine will devote an eight-page spread to the project, shining the spotlight once again on Myrtle.

So far the publicity has garnered a lot of attention for the young developer. In addition to giving numerous interviews to local radio, television, and newspapers, Myrtle has appeared in relevant national trade magazines. Stuart Cannon, president of the National Builders' Association, read about Myrtle in the last issue of *The Nation's Magazine for Builders*. Intrigued, Stuart called Myrtle and invited her to give a presentation to building contractors who would be gathering for their annual national meeting. Scheduled to be held in Kansas City, Missouri, at the end of the year, the meeting would be attended by more than 500 builders and 300 suppliers. When Myrtle learned the meeting's theme—Success Through Environmental Sensibility—she couldn't turn down the opportunity. So she said "yes" to Stuart.

However, Myrtle had never given a speech to a national audience. While she was honored, she was also apprehensive. So she asked her administrative assistant, Dawn Pellegrino, to find the best way to approach the task.

Dawn, who had worked with Myrtle for three years, prided herself on doing a good job, so she started to work on Myrtle's request by learning about presentation strategies.

Dawn called the local university's library and was directed to a resource titled "Presentation Strategies Adopted by *Fortune*'s Top Eight Most Powerful Women in Business."[2] In anticipation of her meeting with Myrtle to talk about the upcoming presentation, Dawn highlighted the article's key findings and transcribed the following notes:

Information for Myrtle's presentation:

The presentations from Fortune's Top 8 Business Women share the following 10 strategies:

1. *An awareness of audience*
2. *A clearly articulated purpose*
3. *An explicit preview or agenda*
4. *Use of transitional sentences*
5. *Internal enumeration*

6. *Support: authorities*
7. *Support: statistics*
8. *Support: examples*
9. *Humor included*
10. *Optimism included*

The women in the study are (1) Carly Fiorina of Hewlett-Packard, (2) Betsy Holden of Kraft Foods, (3) Meg Whitman of eBay, (4) Indra Nooyi of PepsiCo, (5) Andrea Jung of Avon, (6) Anne Mulcahy of Xerox, (7) Karen Katen of Pfizer, and (8) Pat Woertz of ChevronTexaco.

Dawn also transcribed a few excerpts to illustrate each strategy (see Exhibit 1) and then met with Myrtle. Impressed with the information, Myrtle asked Dawn to

1. Draft the remarks, incorporating as many of the strategies as she naturally could.
2. Develop slides and supplements.

From her research, Dawn knew Myrtle would need to articulate a clear purpose, so before the meeting ended, Dawn asked, "What do you want your audience to do or to know?"

Myrtle responded, "I want my audience to understand how mixed-use communities enrich lives and are better for the environment, and—as a result of my presentation—be willing to apply at least some mixed-use concepts to their next project."

Dawn responded, "Well, I think I can start with that. If I have questions, I'll let you know."

Your Audience

Your audience comprises building contractors and suppliers who have gathered for their national annual meeting. How would you characterize building contractors? What is the likely gender split? What educational and experiential interests and expertise do building contractors and suppliers share? What issues are prevalent in the industry today that

---

[2] H. Schultz, "Presentation Strategies Adopted by *Fortune*'s Top Eight Most Powerful Women in Business." Presentation, Association of Business Communication National Convention, Albuquerque, November 2003. This is what we call "shameless self promotion"!

will likely interest suppliers and building contractors? What zoning issues might concern contractors?

Your Task

Once you've answered these and other important questions about the audience, keep your purpose in mind and move on to the content. Do some research to learn what's new in mixed-use communities and environmentally sensitive construction and development practices. Then plug your findings into the presentation outline (available in Chapter 2 "Business Speaking Basics"). In addition, be sure to use the support strategies and slide design strategies covered in Chapter 2.

Nuts and Bolts

- Plan the presentation so it takes up to seven minutes.
- Invite questions at the end.
- Design a handout that enhances the message.
- If your instructor requires you to do so, deliver the presentation.

Exhibit 1

Excerpts from the Presentations

Audience Awareness

Meg Whitman: Now let me talk about how eBay and the strength of our community have built a tremendous marketplace for something near and dear to your hearts—computers and electronics. [Speaking to a convention of computer experts][3]

Pat Woertz: I know this is oil country. But just so there's no misunderstanding: When I speak of "downstream," I'm referring to our traditional refining, marketing, and transportation business. . . . [Speaking to analysts in Texas][4]

Indra Nooyi: First, I want to offer congratulations. When I picked up my *Wall Street Journal* a couple of weeks ago, I read that Tuck again ranked #1 in the survey of business schools. [Speaking at Tuck's Business School][5]

A Clear Purpose

Carly Fiorina: I am here to talk about you. I am here to talk about what we believe is the real agenda in IT, and that is, the "customer's agenda."[6]

---

[3] Meg Whitman. Keynote speech. Comdex Fall 2001 Conference. Chicago, IL, November 14, 2001.

[4] Pat Woertz. Presentation to stockholders. 2003 Annual Meeting. Midland, TX, May 22, 2003.

[5] Indra Nooyi. Remarks at Tuck School of Business. New Hanover, NH, September 23, 2002.

[6] Carly Fiorina. "Return on IT—the Business of Change." Handelsblatt Strategic IT Management Conference. Dusseldorf, Germany, January 28, 2003.

Betsy Holden: [O]ver the next few minutes, we'd like to bring you up-to-date on the state of our business at Kraft.[7]

Anne Mulcahy: What I'd like to do with my time is briefly update you on the state of our business . . . share with you my priorities over the next few years . . . and be presumptuous enough to make a few suggestions to this impressive gathering of public policy makers, thinkers, and advocates—not that I'm drawing any distinction between those who think and those who advocate! And of course, I'll leave plenty of time for dialogue.[8]

Explicit Transitions

Karen Katen: *In other product developments,* earlier this week the FDA approved the antibiotic Zibox, for treatment of diabetic foot infection, which as you know is a difficult condition to treat. . . .[9]

Carly Fiorina: Now, the theme of this conference is all about business performance. And there can be no business performance without trust. And of course, one of the things that has also been on everyone's mind is the issue of trust and corporate governance. And so *let me spend just a few minutes before I close on that topic.*[10]

Internal Lists and Enumeration

Betsy Holden: On the growth side, we expect another billion-dollar-plus year for new products, with continuing focus on the *four high-growth areas* of snacks, beverages, convenient meals, and health and wellness.[11]

Indra Nooyi: I think of them [the following lessons] as *Five Great Lessons from the School of Hard Knocks.*[12]

Support: Authorities

Indra Nooyi: The much-quoted 19th-century British prime minister and author *Benjamin Disraeli* probably said it best: "There is no education like adversity." . . . And in doing so [sharing the following lessons], I hope to disprove a theory set forth some years ago by the great Italian philosopher . . . *Gina Lollibrigida.* Gina

---

[7] Betsy Holden. Business review at annual meeting of stockholders. 2003 Annual Meeting. East Hanover, NJ, April 22, 2003.

[8] Anne Mulcahy. "From Survival to Success: Leading in Turbulent Times." National Chamber Foundation. Washington, DC, April 2, 2003.

[9] Karen Katen. Conference call, second quarter 2003 Pfizer earnings. New York, NY, July 25, 2003.

[10] Carly Fiorina. "Return on IT—the Business of Change." Handelsblatt Strategic IT Management Conference. Dusseldorf, Germany, January 28, 2003.

[11] Betsy Holden. Business review at annual meeting of stockholders. 2003 Annual Meeting. East Hanover, NJ, April 22, 2003.

[12] Indra Nooyi. Remarks at Tuck School of Business. New Hanover, NH, September 23, 2002.

was known for a number of things, one of which was saying, "Whatever we learn we learn too late." On the assumption that she's wrong . . . here's what I have learned. I hope you can put it to use.[13]

Carly Fiorina: Almost exactly 200 years ago, one of my country's greatest presidents, *Thomas Jefferson,* wrote that "given a choice between a government without newspapers, or newspapers without government, I would not hesitate for a moment to choose newspapers without government." Of course, it should be noted that he wrote this before he became president. After serving as president for 8 years, Jefferson wrote that "the man who reads nothing at all is better than the man who reads nothing but newspapers." I'm not sure what brought about this change of heart, but my guess is that it had something to do with the press he received when he pulled off the biggest merger to that point in the history of the United States, also known as the Louisiana Purchase. And of course, you all know our merger created some controversial and—at times—quite colorful press.[14]

Support: Statistics

Meg Whitman: The computer category . . . is on track to generate more than *$1.4 billion* dollars in sales in the U.S. alone—with *$2 billion* worldwide. . . . [Put another way] *2,000 PCs* are bought and sold on the computer site every day.[15]

Pat Woertz: We . . . have more than *26,000 employees* working in the downstream, [her area], which is about half of ChevronTexaco's global workforce. Each day, we manufacture more than *2 million barrels* of refined products in *23 wholly owned* or *joint-venture refineries*. We market through more than *24,000 retail outlets*.[16]

Anne Mulcahy: Let me give you just one example. I'm willing to bet that most of your organizations generate a lot of documents—both paper and electronic. In fact, you are all probably drowning in documents. And I'm also willing to bet that most of your organizations have very little understanding of how much you spend on documents—even though you are focused relentlessly on cost in other areas of your businesses. Would you be shocked to know that the typical organization spends between *5 and 15%* of its annual revenue on documents? To help our customers manage that investment, we do what we call an Office Document Assessment of many of our customers around the world. . . .[17]

---

[13] Indra Nooyi. Remarks at Tuck School of Business. New Hanover, NH, September 23, 2002.

[14] Carly Fiorina. "Return on IT—the Business of Change." Handelsblatt Strategic IT Management Conference. Dusseldorf, Germany, January 28, 2003.

[15] Meg Whitman. Keynote speech. Comdex Fall 2001 Conference. Chicago, IL, November 14, 2001.

[16] Pat Woertz. Presentation to stockholders. 2003 Annual Meeting. Midland, TX, May 22, 2003.

[17] Anne Mulcahy. "From Survival to Success: Leading in Turbulent Times." National Chamber Foundation. Washington, DC, April 2, 2003.

CHAPTER 12

Turn Out the Lights

Chapter Emphasis

- **Structuring a Negative Message**
- **Adopting a Communication Strategy**
- **Adopting an Effective Business Tone**
- **Communicating with Employees**
- **Polishing Presentation Skills**

Rationale

In my experiences of working with professionals at the executive level, nothing is more painful to them than reducing a workforce. Jaime Stefan, VP of Human Resources, Broadline Division, Performance Food Group, the country's third largest supplier of fresh foods to restaurants, hospitals, and schools, has likened the experience to the grieving process. "As a manager, you go through this emotional rollercoaster starting with shock and denial, anger and guilt all while faced with the task of closing a facility, relocating a facility, or letting people go—in some cases, people you've worked with for 20 years; people who have given their all. It's miserable."

To give you a little insight into a situation as emotionally charged as this one, I've included this scenario. It puts the complexity of a communication strategy into the context of job layoffs, and, as such, moves all the way to the right of the "bad news continuum" on p. 77. The scenario raises the "communication bar" because it asks you to face employees via a presentation.

You may want to revisit concepts related to negative news in Chapter 7, presentation skills in Chapter 2, and tone in Chapter 5 before undertaking the assignment.

Turn Out the Lights

Cascade Hills, located 75 miles southwest of Minnesota's state capital, is an idyllic place that embodies most of the characteristics of an all-American town. Indeed, those who venture along the "Mayberry-esque" main street will see the local drugstore, barber shop, and soda shop still serving customers. With its quaint downtown, leafy neighborhoods, and tight-knit community, more than 19,000 residents call Cascade Hills home. However, with a labor force of 8,500 and unemployment hovering around 8 percent, Cascade Hills has recently experienced its share of economic challenges.

That wasn't always the case. In 1972, when Capital Energy Corporation (CEC) decided to expand its Capital Electricity and Light (CEL) division and build a generating facility just outside Cascade Hills, town residents were ecstatic because the energy company would eventually bring hundreds of jobs to the small town. CEC identified the Cascade Hills facility as one the company would use to supplement other CEL plants by adding power during peak demands. Consisting of two steam generation units and two combustion turbine generators, construction on all four units was completed in August 1975 at a cost of more than $60 million. Then in 1999, CEC completed a solar generating unit at the site, which increased the number of employees. (See Exhibit 1 for information about CEC and its corporate structure.)

Exhibit 1

Capital Energy Corporation's Corporate Structure

Description. CEC Corporation is an energy company with interests in both natural gas and electricity. It gathers, processes, stores, transports, and sells natural gas. In addition, the company designs, builds, owns, and operates electric generating facilities. In sum, the company provides reliable energy to millions of customers.

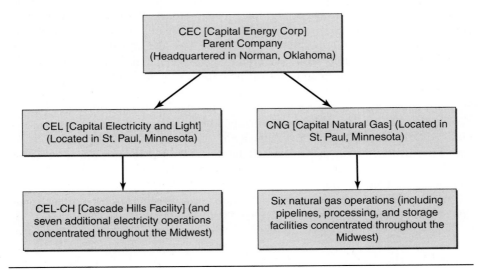

At the beginning of 2003, the Cascade Hills facility, known as Capital Electricity and Light Cascade Hills (CEL-CH), employed more than 350 town residents as technical managers, line and ground technicians, office assistants, building managers, and building engineers. However, CEL-CH was more than a company that provided steady employment; it was a respected corporate citizen in the community. In 1976, CEL-CH donated $5,000 and employee time to install lights at the local baseball stadium; in 1982, it pledged 70 percent of the funds needed to build the new community library; and since the mid-1980s, CEL-CH has awarded college scholarships to the high school's top 10 graduates each year. Last year, Mayor Mike Lopez and local community dignitaries led a special ceremony renaming the village green in honor of the company.

So, in early February this year, when the CEC Board of Directors approved a new restructuring plan that would close the Cascade Hills facility and move 85 of the 350 employees to the company's main operations 75 miles away, the implications for the town would be serious. Moreover, the timing of the closing was less than ideal. CEL had just finished a banner year, with profits at an all-time high. Even so, CEC Corp.—CEL's parent company located just outside Norman, Oklahoma—had experienced severe economic challenges. In fact, CEL-CH would be the third plant targeted for closure in the last 18 months.

After the board approved the restructuring plan, CEL's president India Dale called a meeting of her executive team so they could identify a strategy for announcing the change. (See Exhibit 2 for a list of the executive team members who attended the meeting.)

Exhibit 2

Executive Members at CEL Electricity Who Attended the Meeting Called by India Dale

- Nick Phillips, VP of Asset Performance
- David Harms, VP of Human Resources
- Anne-Marie Holding, VP of Investor Relations
- Randy Setzer, VP of Corporate Communication
- Angela Perrault, CEL's corporate lawyer

At the meeting, India summarized the highlights of the move. The company would phase in the closing over a three-month period starting in mid-April. At this stage, however, no one knew which employees would be offered transfers and which would be let go. Those employees who were given the option of staying with the company at CEL's headquarters would notice no change in salary or benefits. However, transferred workers would need to be aware of a few logistics at CEL's headquarters. Office workers would be assigned to specific desks and offices according to a phase-in plan developed by HR; each would get a four-week notice to make the transition; and each would continue to keep track of hours via the company intranet from computers on their desks. Field workers would also get a four-week notice and would clock in and clock out from one of two computer kiosks in Dispatch Central. Employee parking—for both office and field workers—would be on the southwest corner of the main building, while field workers would have to park their company trucks on the south side, directly behind the field workers' office. (See Exhibit 3.)

Exhibit 3

Layout of CEL Electricity's Main Facilities

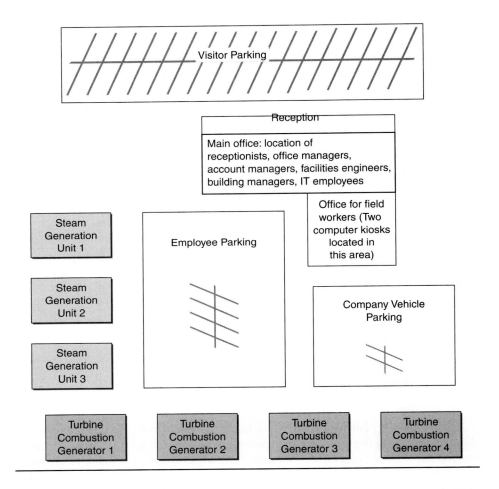

For those employees who would be leaving the company, CEL had arranged to have

- HR staff from headquarters on-site at the CEL-CH facility.
- Outplacement services available on-site from Privileged Placement®.
- Several "Employment Messages Sessions" to focus on cover letter writing, resume writing, and interviewing skills.
- An Employment Security Commission representative on-site one day a week during the transition.

Also at the three-hour meeting, the executive team decided on the following approach:

- The company would make the announcement on Friday, March 5.
- On March 4, the evening before the announcement, India would travel to Cascade Hills to meet with Rob Patel, Facilities Manager, and share the news with him in person.
- After the meeting between Rob and India, all employees would get a telephone message asking them to be in the company cafeteria at 4:00 P.M., March 5, for an important meeting. While that's all the preliminary information employees would get, the executive team agreed that the VP of Asset Performance, Nick Phillips, and a senior representative from HR would lead the face-to-face meeting.
- On March 4, the evening before the employee announcement, shareholders and analysts would get an email message—crafted by Anne-Marie's team—informing them of a Webcast set for 4:30 P.M. (EST) the next afternoon. Shareholders and other interested parties would be able to access the Webcast on March 5 via www.celc.com by selecting the "Investor Relations" link and following the instructions.
- Simultaneous to the employee meeting set for 4:00 P.M., March 5, several additional announcements would go out.
    1. India would call the mayor directly. She had his work, home, and cell numbers.
    2. Staff from Corporate Communication would post a press release to the company Website and contact the regional TV stations, while Randy would call the editor of the *Cascade Hills Gazette* directly.
    3. Angela would contact the appropriate utility regulators. No doubt, the decision to close Cascade Hills would play into any future rate adjustments.
- At 4:30 P.M. on March 5, both India and Anne-Marie would participate in the Webcast for shareholders and analysts. Their goal would be to provide the rationale and financials that drove CEC and CEL's decision to close the Cascade Hills facility.

Your Task

Prepare the presentation to the 350 employees at the Cascade Hills facility announcing the closing. Include PowerPoint slides if you believe you need them. Anticipate questions the audience may have and prepare your responses. Be sure to apply a specific communication strategy to this situation.

Additional Task

Role-play the meeting between India Dale and Rob Patel.

Additional Task

Role-play the telephone conversation between India Dale and Mayor Mike Lopez.

CHAPTER 13

Let's Go Out to Eat

Chapter Emphasis

- **Communicating During a Crisis**
- **Developing a Communication Strategy**
- **Crafting Negative Information**

Rationale

The world of work isn't static from week to week, day to day, or even moment to moment. It changes—sometimes quite unexpectedly, sometimes in a bad way. As a result, you need to be prepared to adapt your communication strategies to reflect these changes. To that end, this scenario gives you the opportunity to experience what it's like to communicate in an unstable environment. That's what NASA had to do when the Space Shuttle *Columbia* tragically exploded on its return to earth on February 1, 2003. That's what the New York Port Authority and Mayor Rudy Giuliani had to do after the disastrous events of September 11, 2001.

Anatomy of a Crisis

According to experts in the field of crisis communication, a crisis is defined as "[a] specific, unexpected, and non-routine event or series of events that create high levels of uncertainty and threaten or are perceived to threaten an organization's high priority goals."[1]

Paul Argenti, professor of Management and Corporate Communication at Tuck School of Business, defines a crisis as "[a] major catastrophe that may occur either naturally or as a result of human error. It can include tangible devastation, such as the destruction of lives or assets, or intangible devastation, such as the loss of an organization's credibility. In the latter case, the loss of credibility may be the result of management's response to tangible devastation or the result of human error."[2]

With that definition, let's look at how to create a workable communication strategy based on the "communication triangle" introduced in Chapter 3. You'll remember that an effective message depends on the interrelationship among the situation, communicator, and audience, as the visual here shows.

---

[1] Matthew W. Seeger, Timothy L. Sellnow, and Robert R. Ullmer, *Communication and Organizational Crisis* (Westport, CT: Praeger Publishers), 2003.

[2] P. Argenti, *Corporate Communication,* 2nd ed. (Boston: McGraw-Hill/Irwin, 1998), p. 214.

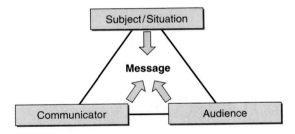

If we apply the generic communication triangle to crisis communication, we get something like the following visual:

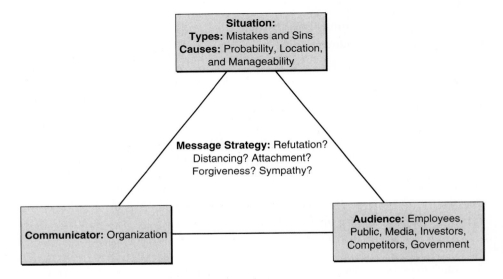

Let's take a look at each component in more detail.

Communicator   While a person communicates on behalf of an organization, the reputation of the organization—how the public, employees, and others perceive that organization—plays the most important role in crisis communication. For example, the rising cost of health care is causing more companies to reduce those benefits. However, because the situation is one that's forced upon companies from external sources, employees may be more willing to perceive the organization as victim rather than victimizer. Indeed, the reputations of tobacco producers and not-for-profits differ, and a communicator needs to take that difference into account when designing a communication strategy.

Situation. Types of Crises   To respond effectively to a crisis, you have to know the types of crises your organization is facing.

- **Mistakes** are unintentional blunders or accidents caused by carelessness in either acts or judgment.

- **Sins** are intentional actions that put the organization or public at risk. Andrew Fastow and Kenneth Lay of Enron, Bernie Ebbers of WorldCom, and Martha Stewart stand as shining examples of corporate sinners.

To put these definitions into context, let's look at several real situations.

- **Alaska Airlines.** This situation is complicated and interesting. Alaska Airlines Flight 261 crashed on January 31, 2000. All 88 people on board died when the MD-80 twin-engine jet en route from Puerto Vallarta, Mexico, to San Francisco crashed upside down into the Pacific Ocean. Excessive wear on the jackscrew—a part that controls a plane's up-and-down movement—caused it to fail. As such, this crisis could be deemed a mistake. However, because the mechanics who worked for the air carrier were being investigated for falsifying maintenance records, the crisis could be deemed a sin.[3]

- **NASA's *Challenger*** accident falls under two categories—sin and mistake—because NASA ignored warnings from the O-ring manufacturer regarding its potential to fail in cold weather. NASA's *Columbia* accident falls under the mistake category because the foam that hit the left wing was unintentional—we'll have to see whether allowing the shuttle to re-enter the earth's atmosphere under those conditions falls under the sin category.

- **The Sasser computer virus,** created by 18-year-old Sven Jaschan and released in 2004, falls under the sin category. His work infected the computers at the U.K. Coastguard, hospitals in Hong Kong, banks in Finland, and the European Commission's Headquarters in Brussels.

Situation. Causes of Crises   Your audience—employees, shareholders, and the general public—will react to an organization's crisis based on what they perceive to be the *cause* of that crisis. The *cause* of a crisis evolves from its probability, location, and manageability.

- **Probability** Is the cause of a crisis always present or does it vary over time? How likely is the threat based on what we know today? The probability of equipment malfunction in jetliners without maintenance is high. So if an airline doesn't have a maintenance plan to protect passengers and crew members, the organization is perceived as negligent when crashes occur due to preventable mechanical failures. The probability of hijackers crashing planes into tall buildings was low on September 10, 2001. Thus, American and United Airlines were perceived as victims. To put this dichotomy into perspective, more people flew American Airlines after 9/11 than flew ValueJet (which changed its name to AirTran) after one of its jets crashed into the Everglades in 1999. So the probability of a crisis is one important factor in anticipating public reaction to that crisis.

- **Location** Is the crisis located internally or externally? While every organization can implement internal safety measures, organizations have less control over

---

[3] Henry K. Lee, "U.S. Reopens Alaska Air Crash Probe," *San Francisco Chronicle,* March 13, 2003; Scott Thurston, "Airlines Ground Suspect Planes," *Atlanta Journal and Constitution,* February 12, 2000.

external crises. For example, if a December hurricane hits the east coast, the location is external, and an organization has little control over that crisis. However, if in December the power company doesn't have a plan to respond efficiently to power outages as a result of typical winter storms, then the crisis is an internal one. An organization's constituencies are typically more forgiving if they perceive the crisis as external.

- **Manageability** Finally, how much can an organization manage the threat of or prepare for a crisis? If the manageability is high and an organization chooses not to use that manageability to prepare for crises, the organization's constituencies will react negatively. In 1991, 25 Imperial Foods employees died as a result of a fire at the chicken processing plant in Hamlet, North Carolina. Victims weren't able to escape from the burning building because the owners had locked the exit doors. If we want to give the owners the benefit of the doubt and claim that the probability of the crisis was low, fine. However, the location of this crisis was internal, and its manageability was high. As such, public reaction was negative, and the owners both received hefty prison sentences.

Message Strategies   So once you understand the types of crises and how audiences judge crises based on probability, location, and manageability, you're ready to consider various response strategies. Coombs's categories are useful:[4]

- **Refutation** seeks to eliminate the crisis. In the widely publicized trial of Martha Stewart, a former lawyer for her company testified that he recommended she deny any wrongdoing. And Stewart's publicist, Susan Magrino, said, "Martha Stewart did not receive any non-public information regarding ImClone prior to her sale of a small number of shares. Her transaction was entirely lawful."[5] Sometimes, an organization will use refutation with intimidation. This strategy is aggressive and most often includes the threat of legal action against those who reference an organization's crisis—real or perceived. However, if an organization uses refutational strategies supported by the threat of legal action, the organization must be absolutely sure it is correct that a crisis does not exist. In Stewart's case, refutation did not work. She was found guilty and sentenced to five months in prison.

- **Distancing** acknowledges the crisis and attempts to create public acceptance of the crisis while weakening the linkage between the crisis and the organization. On February 26, 2004, Bridgestone/Firestone announced its second major tire recall within four years because of fatalities in Ford SUVs. A link to "Voluntary Safety Campaign Frequently Asked Questions (FAQs)" acknowledged "there could be an issue with these tires." However, the same document used a distancing strategy with the following statement: "We believe if these tires are properly inflated and

---

[4] T.W. Coombs, "Choosing the Right Words: The Development of Guidelines for the Selection of the 'Appropriate' Response Strategies," *Management Communication Quarterly* 8, no. 4 (1995), p. 447.

[5] Greg Farrell, "Witness: Stewart Urged to Deny Wrongdoing," *USA Today,* February 19, 2004.

maintained and if the vehicle is operated within its load carrying capacity, they will perform very well."[6]

- **Attachment** seeks to gain approval for the organization during a crisis. For example, Nike was accused of unfair labor practices by labor activist Marc Kasky. However, when Nike agreed on September 11, 2003, to donate $1.5 million to the Fair Labor Association to help develop worker training programs and increase monitoring of international labor standards, it successfully used attachment strategies to minimize the negative effective of this crisis. Indeed, attachment strategies attempt to bolster the organization's attributes and reputation.

- **Forgiveness** seeks to win forgiveness from the public and to create an acceptance for the crisis. Under this category, three subcategories emerge. They are remediation, repentance, and rectification.

  - **Remediation**—offers some sort of compensation for victims to lessen negative feelings toward the organization. This response strategy is tangible and can reach hundreds of millions of dollars in settlements from corporations to victims.

  - **Repentance**—simply asks for forgiveness. As the organization or its leaders ask for forgiveness, negativity decreases in the public's mind. In response to the Iraqi prisoner abuse scandal Abu Ghraib prison that broke in late April 2004, Defense Secretary Donald Rumsfeld appeared before members of Congress. There, he apologized for the mistreatment of Iraqi prisoners of war: "Our country had an obligation to treat them right. We didn't, and that was wrong. So to those Iraqis who were mistreated by members of the U.S. armed forces, I offer my deepest apology."[7]

  - **Rectification**—takes action so as to prevent recurrence of the crisis. After the crash of Alaska Airlines Flight 261, the airline canceled a dozen flights to repeat tail inspections on the carrier's fleet.

- **Sympathy** seeks to portray itself as a victim. The classic example here is the Johnson & Johnson Tylenol crisis in which seven people died from ingesting Extra-Strength Tylenol that was laced with cyanide. This response strategy works particularly well when an organization is a victim of terrorism.

These components are complex and interdependent. An internal crisis can be classified as a sin, while manageability can be classified as low. This combination typically occurs in, for example, employee sabotage. Indeed, understanding this interdependent complexity becomes important when formulating a communication strategy.

The following scenario gives you practice responding to a real crisis faced in the restaurant industry. As you read it, keep in mind the type of crisis that unfolds, the organization's culture, and its responses to the crisis as it unfolds.

---

[6] Voluntary Safety Campaign Frequently Asked Questions (FAQs) (February 26, 2004). http://www.bridgestone-firestone.com/news/news_index.asp?id+stx/040226a_faq.

[7] George Edmonson and Eunice Moscoso, "More Shocks Ahead; Rumsfeld Apologizes for Mistreatment of Iraqi Prisoners," *Atlanta Journal-Constitution,* May 8, 2004.

Background

According to the National Restaurant Association, "[O]n a typical day in 2004, the restaurant industry will post average sales of more than $1.2 billion."[8] That's a lot of eating out! With all the demands on our time, it's nice to have someone else shop, cook, and wash the dishes. Sometimes, however, leaving the culinary chores to others can come with risks. According to the Centers for Disease Control, "[F]oodborne diseases cause approximately 76 million illnesses, 325,000 hospitalizations, and 5,000 deaths in the United States each year."[9] One such disease, hepatitis A, is transmitted via fecal matter in food and water when people don't wash their hands after bathroom breaks. Indeed, foodborne illnesses can be a serious threat to the public health. That's what happened in the fall of 2003 to patrons who dined at Chi-Chi's restaurant[10] in Beaver County, Pennsylvania.

Scenario

Here's a timeline detailing the events as they unfolded.

First Week of October 2003   People dined at ChiChi's in the Beaver Valley Mall, a restaurant 25 miles northwest of Pittsburgh.

Tuesday, October 28   Two patients were diagnosed in the local emergency room with hepatitis A; later that day, four more patients were diagnosed with hepatitis A at Beaver's Medical Center. Dr. Marcus Eubanks was the ER physician on call.

Saturday, November 1   Dr. Andrew Weltman, public health physician with the Pennsylvania State Department of Health living in Harrisburg,[11] got a message at 7:00 A.M. about the increasing number of patients being seen with hepatitis A. By the end of the day, inspectors from the state Department of Agriculture had visited the restaurant and learned that several workers were also sick.

Over the Weekend   The number of confirmed and probable cases of hepatitis A continued to grow; however, the health department didn't go public with the information until it had completed plans to set up a clinic in the area. One of the sticking points involved buying enough immune globulin, which can provide temporary immunity to hepatitis A. However, this medicine wasn't readily stocked in doctors' offices or hospitals.

Monday, November 3   The Pennsylvania Department of Health issued a news release about the problem.

---

[8] 2004 Restaurant Industry Forecast Executive Summary. National Restaurant Association. www.restaurant.org, p. 2. Accessed May 11, 2004.

[9] Paul S. Mead, et al., "Food-Related Illness and Death in the United States." *CDC Emerging Infectious Diseases.* September–October 1999. www.cdc.gov/ncidod/eid/vol5no5/mead.htm. Accessed May 11, 2004.

[10] Chi-Chi's is a casual Mexican restaurant chain with 100 company-owned stores and headquartered in Louisville, KY.

[11] Four hours east of Beaver, PA.

Wednesday, November 5   The state started to offer antibody inoculations in a clinic it had set up at Beaver County Community College, where 3,000 people got immune globulin shots. At this point in the events, evidence suggests that worker hygiene at the restaurant may have caused the outbreak.

Friday, November 7   Jeff Cook was the first person to die. Chi-Chi's issued a press release. (See Exhibit 1 for a copy of the press release.)

Exhibit 1

November 7, 2003, Press Release

Chi-Chi's Comments on Hepatitis A Outbreak in Beaver County, PA

LOUISVILLE, KY, November 7—Chi-Chi's, Inc., a Mexican restaurant chain headquartered in Louisville, Kentucky, expressed its concerns today regarding the recent outbreak of Hepatitis A in Beaver County, Pennsylvania.

According to the Center for Disease Control of Atlanta, Georgia (CDC), as many as 127 area residents may have become ill with Hepatitis A as of the morning of November 7, 2003. The Company today confirmed that six employees at its Chi-Chi's restaurant in the Beaver Valley Mall are among those area residents who tested positive for Hepatitis A and these employees are under medical supervision.

Upon learning that the restaurant may have been a contributing factor to the outbreak, the Company voluntarily closed the location and retained a qualified medical expert to investigate the cause of the illness, supervise testing and medical treatment of the employees, and to confirm that the food handling and hygiene policies at the restaurant chain take every precaution against the spread of food-borne illnesses. Chi-Chi's is working actively with the Pennsylvania Department of Health to ensure that the location is thoroughly sanitized and that all employees are cleared of any possible infection before returning to work. The Company's medical advisor is also working closely with the CDC to determine the source of the infection.

Bill Zavertnik, Chi-Chi's Chief Operating Officer, commented: "Chi-Chi's deeply regrets the recent spread of Hepatitis A in the Beaver Valley area of Pennsylvania. Over the years, our Company has developed and enacted food safety programs that place the Company in the top percentile of national restaurant chains in the promotion and enforcement of the highest standards of health and hygiene. Our hearts go out to the families that have been impacted.

"The origin of this outbreak is still under investigation. We do know that several Chi-Chi's employees have become ill with Hepatitis A. We have clear and long-standing policies that prohibit employees from working while sick. However, given my understanding of the incubation period, several employees may have worked not knowing that they had been infected or could pass on that infection to others.

"We sincerely apologize to all of our loyal customers and want to inform the community that Chi-Chi's will do everything within our power to make sure that our patrons continue to enjoy a healthful and rewarding dining experience and that our employees have a safe and sanitized working atmosphere. The Beaver Valley Chi-Chi's has received excellent scores on its most recent health department inspections, scoring 94 and 95 out of 100 in 2003 and 2002, respectively. We intend to fully investigate the origin of this outbreak and ensure that Chi-Chi's industry leading sanitation policies are followed to the letter at every single Chi-Chi's location."

About Hepatitis A

Hepatitis A is an infectious disease caused by the Hepatitis A virus. According to the CDC, approximately 1/3 of Americans had evidence of past Hepatitis A infection, which provides immunity to the disease. Unlike other strains of Hepatitis, there is no chronic (long-term) infection with Hepatitis A.

Further information about Hepatitis A can be found at the CDC website at www.cdc.gov. Anyone who suspects they have been exposed to the virus should contact their physician.

The CDC website states: "Persons with Hepatitis A virus infection may not have any signs or symptoms of the disease. Older persons are more likely to have symptoms than children. If symptoms are present, they usually occur abruptly and may include fever, tiredness, loss of appetite, nausea, abdominal discomfort, dark urine, and jaundice (yellowing of the skin and eyes)."

Persons who suspect they have come into contact with the Hepatitis A virus can be treated with immune globulin. The CDC describes immune globulin as "a preparation of antibodies that can be given before exposure for short-term protection against Hepatitis A and for persons who have already been exposed to Hepatitis A virus. Immune globulin must be given within 2 weeks after exposure to Hepatitis A virus for maximum protection."

November 9   The State Department of Health closed its hepatitis clinic at Beaver County Community College.

November 10   Up to this point, the State Department of Health had confirmed 240 cases of hepatitis A. In addition, 8,884 people were screened for exposure and 8,230 received immune globulin shots. The State Department of Health picked up the tab.

November 11   On this date, state officials said they didn't know whether worker hygiene or a contaminated shipment of food was to blame. State Health Department spokesman, Richard McGarvey, said,

> What it comes back to is, What was the transmission route? Was it someone with poor hygiene? Was it a food product coming into Chi-Chi's? Hopefully, we're going to nail that down pretty soon.

Investigators believed the contamination was more likely a problem with food-worker hygiene than a food item that had arrived at the restaurant already contaminated.

Chi-Chi's scheduled a press conference for the next day, November 12, at 3:00 P.M.

Later on November 11   After consulting with the Centers for Disease Control in Atlanta and the Pennsylvania State Department of Health, Chi-Chi's announced its intention to delay the press conference. The press conference would be held as soon as the Company had more definitive data as to the source of the outbreak. (See Exhibit 2 for a transcript of the press release.)

Exhibit 2

November 11, 2003, Press Release

Chi-Chi's, Inc. Provides Additional Information on Hepatitis A Outbreak

Planned press conference is postponed; re-opening date yet to be determined

LOUISVILLE, KY, November 11th—Chi-Chi's, Inc., a Mexican restaurant chain headquartered in Louisville, Kentucky, today announced that after consultation with the Center for Disease Control in Atlanta, Georgia (CDC), and the Pennsylvania Department of Health, the decision has been made to delay the press conference at which the Company planned to address the recent outbreak of Hepatitis A in the Beaver Valley area. The press conference, which was originally scheduled for Wednesday, November 12th at 3 P.M., will now be held as soon as the Company has more definitive data as to the source of the outbreak.

Commenting on recent developments, Bill Zavertnik, Chief Operating Officer of Chi-Chi's, Inc., said, "We realize that there has been a tremendous amount of speculation and confusion about this outbreak in the community. We at Chi-Chi's share the community's concerns regarding the outbreak and we would like to take this opportunity to clarify some of the issues as we understand them.

"Over the past 10 days, our managers and the Company's medical advisor have been working tirelessly with the CDC, the Pennsylvania Department of Health to attempt to identify the source of the outbreak. According to the Pennsylvania Department of Health, as of this evening, Tuesday November 11th, the number of confirmed positive Hepatitis A cases stands at 300. Based on our discussions with the public health authorities, the source of the outbreak has not yet been determined. We would like to emphasize that this remains an isolated incident and that none of the other restaurants in the chain have been affected by this outbreak.

"We've spent nearly thirty years here at Chi-Chi's building a national reputation for providing quality Mexican food in a fun and safe environment. Our health and safety protocols are consistent with the highest standards of the best restaurant chains in America. We are proud of our record of educating and training our staff in correct and proper food safety hygiene, including hand washing and food preparation procedures. In the last two years, our Beaver Valley location has had four separate health inspections and we have scored 94, 95, 98 and 100 out of a possible 100.

"I'd like to stress that we are committed to getting to the bottom of these issues and ensuring that our guests continue to have an enjoyable and safe dining experience and that none of our other restaurants are involved."

November 12   By now, health officials confirm 410 cases of hepatitis A. And by this time, green onions are suspected as the source of the outbreak. In a press release, Chi-Chi's stated it decided to remove the green onions voluntarily. (See Exhibit 3 for a transcript of the press release.)

Exhibit 3

November 12, 2003, Press Release

Chi-Chi's, Inc. Removes Green Onions from Entire Restaurant Chain

Voluntary move made from "abundance of caution"; no other Chi-Chi's restaurants involved in outbreak

LOUISVILLE, KY, November 12th—Chi-Chi's, Inc., a Mexican restaurant chain headquartered in Louisville, Kentucky, today announced that the Company has decided to voluntarily remove green onions from every menu item at every location in the Chi-Chi's restaurant chain.

While there has been no determination of the source of the recent outbreak of Hepatitis A in the Beaver Valley area, officials with the public health authorities have indicated that some product or ingredients are being focused on as possible sources of Hepatitis A contamination.

"Our decision today reflects the fact that contaminated green onions are the prime suspect of recent Hepatitis A outbreaks in various other states. Our primary concern has been and continues to be to protect the health, safety and well being of our guests, our employees and the local community," said Bill Zavertnik, Chief Operating Officer of Chi-Chi's, Inc.

"We have no definitive information that green onions were involved in this outbreak. But out of an abundance of caution we have decided to remove this ingredient from our menu, including its use as a garnish, in salsa and cooked dishes."

The Company reiterated that no Chi-Chi's location outside of the Beaver Valley location has been involved in the Hepatitis A outbreak.

November 13   The manager at another Chi-Chi's in the area said business has been slow since the hepatitis A outbreak at the Beaver Valley Mall. But he indicated there's nothing to worry about at any of the other 19 Chi-Chi's in Pennsylvania. "Believe you me, we're on top of everything more than ever with health and safety stuff," said John Crowley. The only response from the company so far had been in the form of prepared news releases that indicated it was cooperating with the health department. As far as the company's public image, there hadn't been one up to this point.

November 15   To date, 510 people had been infected with hepatitis A and three people had died. A Chi-Chi's executive said the company had adopted "extraordinary measures" companywide in an effort to prevent similar outbreaks elsewhere. These measures included keeping illness logs for employees and asking workers to sign "wellness statements" asserting they were not ill.

According to Bill Zavertnik, Chi-Chi's COO and a Pennsylvanian by birth, all 60 employees of that restaurant would remain under medical supervision until each had been medically cleared. To date, 11 employees tested positive for hepatitis. Zavertnik also said that Chi-Chi's food purchasers were cooperating with investigators to identify the source of the outbreak, and the company hired an epidemiologist to work with the Federal Centers for Disease Control and the Pennsylvania Department of Health.[12] Several lawsuits were filed against Chi-Chi's; however, Zavertnik would not comment on those lawsuits. Once again, health officials suspected the green onions.

November 18 The FDA advised consumers concerned about the possibility of contracting hepatitis A to cook green onions thoroughly and avoid eating them raw or lightly cooked in restaurants. Contaminated green onions were linked to several outbreaks in Atlanta and Macon, Georgia, and in Asheville, North Carolina. Green onions were still thought to be a possible source of the Pennsylvania Chi-Chi's outbreak.

November 21 The FDA stopped allowing the sale of green onions from three Mexican firms because their produce was linked to hepatitis outbreaks. At this point, no one was sure whether one of these Mexican firms supplied the Beaver Valley Mall Chi-Chi's. To date, a total of 540 employees and customers were confirmed to have hepatitis A.

For years, the FDA had ignored warning signs that green onions were a threat to food safety, according to some food safety experts. Dr. Bob Brackett, the FDA's director of food safety and security, said new bioterrorism laws going into effect would strengthen the agency's ability to police produce. According to Brackett, starting December 12, 2003, any companies exporting food to the United States would have to give prior notice to the FDA about when and where the shipment would be crossing the border.

Later that day, health officials confirmed 575 cases of hepatitis A. Chi-Chi's posted a press release on its Web site announcing it had established a toll-free number inviting all customers or employees affected by the outbreak to contact the company. To begin rebuilding trust, Chi-Chi's addressed what it had done for sick customers and employees. (See Exhibit 4 for a transcript of this press release.)

Exhibit 4

November 21, 2003, Press Release

Chi-Chi's, Inc. Comments on Recent Developments in Hepatitis A Investigation and Updates Beaver Valley Community on Outreach Efforts

Toll free number for affected guests and employees at 1-800-328-7761 (9:30 A.M. to 9:00 P.M. EST)

LOUISVILLE, KY, November 21—Chi-Chi's, Inc., a Mexican restaurant chain headquartered in Louisville, Kentucky, today commented on the recent developments in the investigation of the Hepatitis A outbreak in Beaver Valley and announced the start of an outreach effort to the Beaver Valley community.

The Company has established a toll free number (**1-800-328-7761**) to enable all customers or employees affected by the outbreak or having questions or concerns regarding Hepatitis A to contact Chi-Chi's. The Company received approval today from

---

[12] Interview with Hugh Hilton, CEO, Prandium Corp., parent company to Chi-Chi's. September 22, 2004.

the U.S. Bankruptcy Court to proceed with a plan to begin to respond to the needs of affected customers. "Chi Chi's is deeply concerned about the effects of this incident on our guests, our employees and the Beaver Valley community," said Bill Zavertnik, COO for Chi-Chi's, Inc. "From the onset, we have been working hand-in-hand with the public health authorities to identify the origin of this outbreak. And we have taken every possible step to ensure the health and safety of our guests and our employees.

"We learned this morning that the public health authorities have made a preliminary determination that a shipment of green onions was the likely origin of this outbreak, which has infected over 500 people in the region, including 13 Chi-Chi's employees. We are gratified by the comments made at today's news conference by the health authorities. They confirmed that Chi-Chi's employees were not the source of this incident, that there was nothing we could have done to prevent the outbreak, and that this is an isolated incident.

"As soon as there was a suspicion of green onions being involved, Chi-Chi's removed them from our entire chain. There is currently no industry-accepted means of testing produce for Hepatitis A virus. And there is no effective way to wash Hepatitis A off of green onions, as the public health authorities have confirmed. We support the efforts of the FDA, CDC and the Health Department to address the underlying causes of this event. And we want the community to know that we have spared no effort to respond to this incident."

Chi Chi's efforts to date include:

- Working with the Pennsylvania Department of Health, the Center for Disease Control (CDC), and the FDA to ensure the safety of our guests and employees and providing these authorities with on-going assistance in their investigation of the Hepatitis A incident.
- Inoculation, testing, and precautionary measures for all Chi Chi's Beaver Valley employees.
- Voluntary closure of the restaurant at the Beaver Valley Mall until at least January 2, 2004. The closure will extend at least ten days beyond the maximum incubation period of Hepatitis A and provide the health authorities with a "controlled environment" in which to conduct their investigations.
- Providing financial support to all of the employees who were employed at this restaurant during the period of closure and requesting that they not seek employment elsewhere.
- Providing financial assistance, which may include reimbursement of medical expenses and lost wages, to Chi-Chi's guests who dined at the Beaver Valley Mall location and may have been affected by this incident.

"Chi-Chi's has spent thirty years building a reputation as an industry leader in the area of food safety. We sincerely regret that any of our guests or employees became ill after eating at our Beaver Valley restaurant," said Zavertnik. "We are working diligently to respond to all persons that have been affected by this incident."

"The entire Chi-Chi's team is committed to rebuilding the trust of the community. We hope that our guests will take advantage of the outreach effort and use the 1-800 number to address questions and concerns they may have and request our assistance.

"We would like all of our customers to know that we will do everything possible to continue to provide them with great food and a safe and enjoyable dining experience," Zavertnik concluded.

November 22   According to the Centers for Disease Control, contaminated green onions almost certainly caused the outbreak.

December 1   Lawsuits against Chi-Chi's were dismissed because the company could not have done anything to prevent the outbreak. According to COO Bill Zavertnik,

> We are pleased to learn that these lawsuits have been dismissed. This action confirms our belief that Chi-Chi's could not have done anything to prevent such an outbreak from occurring. However, we are deeply concerned with the impact this incident has had on our guests and employees, and we are committed to rebuilding the trust of the community.

To demonstrate the company's ongoing efforts on behalf of its customers and employees, Mr. Zavertnik invited those affected by the outbreak to call the company's 800 number. (See Exhibit 5 for entire transcript of press release.)

Exhibit 5

December 1, 2003, Press Release

FOR IMMEDIATE RELEASE
Chi-Chi's, Inc. Comments on the Dismissal of Three Lawsuits

Toll free number for affected guests and employees remains open

LOUISVILLE, KY, December 1—Chi-Chi's, Inc., a Mexican restaurant chain headquartered in Louisville, Kentucky, today commented on the dismissal of three lawsuits, previously filed against the Company by the law firm of Marler Clark, in connection with the Hepatitis A outbreak in Beaver Valley.

"Last week, public health authorities determined that a shipment of contaminated green onions to a Chi-Chi's restaurant from an outside supplier was the source of this outbreak," stated attorney William Marler. "For that reason, we have decided to dismiss the lawsuits against Chi-Chi's, and instead have filed a lawsuit against suppliers of Hepatitis A green onions that have been implicated by the FDA and CDC as the source."

Chi-Chi's continues to offer its toll free number (**1-800-328-7761**) to enable all customers or employees affected by the outbreak or having questions or concerns regarding Hepatitis A to contact the company. Last week, Chi-Chi's received approval from the U.S. Bankruptcy Court to proceed with a plan to respond to the needs of affected customers with the reimbursement of medical expenses and lost wages.

"We are pleased to learn that these lawsuits have been dismissed," said Bill Zavertnik, COO for Chi-Chi's, Inc. "This action confirms our belief that Chi-Chi's could not have done anything to prevent such an outbreak from occurring. However, we are deeply concerned with the impact this incident has had on our guests and employees and we are committed to rebuilding the trust of the community. We hope that our guests will take advantage of the outreach effort and use the 1-800 number to address questions and concerns they may have and request our assistance."

Answer the Following Questions

1. What type of crisis is Chi-Chi's facing?

2. What is the cause of the crisis? How probable is it? How manageable is it? Where is it located?

3. Evaluate the communication strategy to date. How effective do you think it's been with the public? What, if anything, would you have done differently?

Assignment

Your Role

Head of Corporate Communications.

Your Task

Given the type and cause of the hepatitis outbreak, write a message to employees at the Beaver store updating them on the situation, reassuring them about what the company is doing, and thanking them for their efforts. Decide whether to distribute the message to employees at the store or send the message to their home addresses.

Write a letter to the Beaver County community updating them on the situation and reassuring them about what the company is doing. Decide whether or not to include persuasive strategies to entice diners back to the restaurant. You'll publish the letter in the local newspaper, *The Beaver County Times.*

Prepare a five-minute statement to the press updating them on the situation and reassuring them about what the company is doing. Decide whether you want to focus on what Chi-Chi's has done and is continuing to do about the situation or whether you want to focus on the green onions. Decide also whether you want to answer questions.

Your Audience

The public (past and potential customers), the press, and investors.

Post script: Operating under bankruptcy protection at the time of the outbreak, Chi-Chi's assets were purchased by Outback Steakhouse on August 4, 2004.

CHAPTER 14

District of Columbia Water and Sewer Authority— Communicating Health Hazards to the Public

Chapter Emphasis

- **Communicating during a Crisis**
- **Developing a Communication Strategy**

  "When you turn on the tap, you expect pure drinking water.
  And you expect that your public water utility will uphold that expectation."
  —Resident, District of Columbia

Background

Lead occurs naturally in the environment. As a malleable and rather inexpensive metal, lead has had many uses throughout history. Ancient civilizations, for example, used lead in makeup, food, paint, pots and pans, and coins. The Romans used lead as an additive in wine and for the pipes that supplied water to the city and surrounding area. Gutenberg's printing press in 15th-century Germany relied on lead for its movable type. And in the early 17th century, Virginia colonists mined lead. Indeed, lead has played an important— but harmful—role throughout the ages.

Note: This scenario presents a serious public health crisis and challenges you to respond appropriately. To prepare yourself to handle this volatile situation successfully, be sure you're familiar with the "Rationale" and "Anatomy of a Crisis" sections presented in Chapter 13.

When humans ingest or inhale lead, they can suffer significant health consequences. In the early stages of lead exposure, people may experience fatigue, irritabil-
ity, loss of appetite, stomach discomfort, a reduced attention span, and insomnia. If not
treated, lead poisoning can result in nerve damage, reproductive problems, and increased blood pressure in adults. In children, lead poisoning can cause brain damage,
mental retardation, liver and kidney damage, and in extreme cases, death.[1] In an effort
to reduce lead ingestion, many states have banned lead pipes in new construction.

In 1992, to protect the public further from this health hazard, the Environmental
Protection Agency (EPA) established a regulation requiring municipal water suppliers
to sample water from household taps twice a year and to analyze those samples for lead
content. So today, if the lead content is above 15 ppb (parts per billion) in more than
10 percent of all homes tested, the utility needs to monitor the contaminant twice a year
and take steps to reduce the amount of lead, while informing the public. In fact, the EPA
has published guidelines on how a water supplier must educate the public:[2]

Public Education

A water supplier that exceeds the lead [limits] . . . is required to conduct a public education
program. . . . This program requires suppliers to:

Insert notices in each customer's utility bill providing background information on the
rule, health effects of lead, how lead gets into drinking water, and steps customers can take
to reduce their exposure to lead in drinking water; the bill must also provide an alert on the
face of the bill itself stating that some homes in the community have elevated lead levels in
their drinking water and encourage consumers to read the enclosed public notice;

Submit information contained in the public notice . . . to the editorial departments of
the major daily and weekly newspapers circulated within the community; and

Submit public service announcements to at least five of the radio stations and
television stations with the largest broadcast audiences in the community.

So it is somewhat surprising that the District of Columbia's Water and Sewer Authority
(DCWASA) kept quiet when it discovered lead in 53 houses between July 2001 and
June 2002. That strategy culminated on March 5, 2004, when executives representing
both DCWASA and the EPA appeared before the House Committee on Government Reform Oversight for a hearing titled "Public Confidence, Down the Drain: The Federal
Role in Ensuring Safe Drinking Water in the District of Columbia." To reconstruct many
of the events leading up to that hearing, a timeline follows.

Timeline[3]

July 2001 to June 2002   DCWASA officials are aware of lead contamination in city
water because random tests on 53 houses reveal lead in the water.

---

[1] Environmental Protection Agency (n.d.) http://www.epa.gov/superfund/programs/lead/health.htm.
Accessed March 22, 2004.

[2] Environment Protection Agency (n.d.) http://www.epa.gov/dclead/oversight.htm#education. Accessed
August 31, 2004.

[3] Timeline constructed from DCWASA's Web site (http://www.dcwasa.com/news/listings/alert), the EPA's
Web site (www.epa.gov/region03), a transcript from *NPR,* and articles from *The Washington Post.*

June 21, 2002   Letter sent to customers informing them "Your Drinking Water Has Met or Surpassed All Federal Standards Everyday in 2001." According to general manager Jerry N. Johnson, "We are once again proud to report that Washington, DC's drinking water met or surpassed all requirements of the federal Safe Drinking Water Act (SDWA) every single day in 2001."

August 2002   Lead problem noted in report to EPA. DCWASA begins to comply with EPA guidelines by replacing pipes. DCWASA asks residents to have their water tested voluntarily without telling residents they might be at risk.

Fall 2002   EPA officials tell DCWASA that it has until December 31, 2003, to replace 7 percent of lead pipes.

October 2002   DCWASA mails an 11-page brochure to every customer in the city about the dangers of lead. On page 10, one paragraph notes that during DCWASA's "last sampling program in the summer of 2001 and June 2002 some . . . homes tested above 15 ppb." That statement is the only indication that DCWASA had discovered a problem.

February 2003   DCWASA mails a letter to all 13 D.C. council members noting that initial tests from the sampling program found water with lead levels that exceeded the EPA's limit.

June 2003   The EPA tells DCWASA that it had made a mistake in telling the water company it has until December 31, 2003, to replace 7 percent of lead pipes; the new compliance date is September 30, 2003.

Summer 2003   DCWASA decides—with EPA approval—to expand testing in order to find approximately 1,200 homes with no lead contamination. With this approach, DCWASA can satisfy EPA lead safety requirements without replacing lead pipes. DCWASA offers payments of $25 and $50 to entice customers to participate in the tests. More than 6,000 residences participate. These tests show that two-thirds of the 6,118 residences had water that exceeded the lead limit of 15 ppb set by the EPA in 1991. And 157 homes tested above 300 ppb. Still, the total number of houses in the DC area was within normal limits, and this number was enough to stall widespread pipe replacement. By law if 10% or fewer homes test above 15 ppb, DCWASA does not need to inform the public at large.

November 2003   DCWASA officials mail results to homeowners who participated in the sampling program.

December 2003   A meeting is announced in community newspapers and on DCWASA's Web site "to discuss and solicit public comments on DCWASA's Safe Drinking Water Act projects." Notice of meeting does not state that lead had been found in tap water. Two Georgetown residents attend. DCWASA spokesman Johnnie Hemphill says, "We're . . . disappointed at the turnout."

DCWASA chief engineer Michael Marcotte says the agency didn't get a handle on the extent of the problem until now. Marcotte: "If we really had wished to manage the data, what we would have done is taken that report . . . and buried it. And we didn't do that. We shared it with people. Frankly, we were still trying to figure out what it means to us and what we need to do moving forward."

During 2003   DCWASA replaced 400 lead pipes at a cost of $2 million.

January 31, 2004   Several D.C. City Council Members, including Mayor Anthony A. Williams (D), are unaware of the lead problem. They learn of it from the *Washington Post*'s article today.

February 1, 2004   D.C. council member Carol Schwartz (R-At Large), head of the council's Committee on Public Works and the Environment, said, "I'm furious about the fact we did not know about this. I want to find out what they know, when they knew it, and what they're going to do about it."

Glenn Gerstell, chairman of DCWASA's 11-member board of directors, says, "Could we be more aggressive reaching out? Maybe so. That's something the board should look at. We're always eager to improve operations. But I want to negate any suggestion whatsoever we are attempting to minimize or downplay or sweep this under the rug. Any news conference would have been an unsatisfactory news conference. We did not know what [the contamination] was due to scientifically or where it was coming from or how many homes were involved. We need more tests. A news conference would have raised a lot of questions and provided no answers at that time."

February 2, 2004   DCWASA posts a "Lead Services Update" in both English and Spanish to its Web site. "In recent months these sample tests, as well as more comprehensive tests undertaken by DCWASA, indicate some, but not all, households with lead service lines may have a higher lead concentration than previously experienced. . . . DCWASA, as required by federal regulation, notifies residents at the identified property that they may experience an increase of lead levels in their drinking water. Special efforts will continue to be made to address the needs of lead service lines about this issue."

February 4, 2004   The D.C. council holds an emergency hearing. A woman in her eighth month of pregnancy testifies that throughout her pregnancy she had been carefully following all of her physician's instructions: she drank no alcohol, didn't smoke, ate right, took her vitamins, and drank lots of tap water, which her doctor had recommended because it contains fluoride and minerals. In September 2003, DCWASA tested her water. In early January, DCWASA informed her by mail the water had extremely high lead levels (more than 20 times the EPA level). In that letter, DCWASA did not recommend that she stop drinking the water.

February 6, 2004   DCWASA announces it has raised this year's budget from $10 million to $17 million for replacing 1,300 lead service lines. EPA announces it will give an additional $3.7 million to help with the replacement of some of the 23,000 lead service lines. NOTE: EPA officials estimate that replacing all the pipes will cost $300 million to $350 million and take as along as 15 years.

February 8, 2004   Chairman of DCWASA's board of directors, Glenn S. Gerstell, said, "We can't just send guys out with a jackhammer tomorrow and do all of these overnight."

Early February 2004   Concerned citizens are directed to email DCWASA or call its lead hot line.[4]

February 11, 2004   DCWASA officials said they should have done a better job of informing the public when tap water tests in 2002 and 2003 revealed high traces of lead contamination. Glenn S. Gerstell, chairman of the board of directors for DCWASA, said, "Should we have been more explicit and turned up the volume? My answer is yes. I think we have learned a lesson from this."

DCWASA's general manager says the agency did not do more to tell the public about the problems in 2002 because early tests were based on relatively few samples. The agency's low-key response was "out of an abundance of caution and not wanting to cause hysteria."

Mayor Anthony A. Williams said, "The DCWASA board should have been much more aggressive about getting information out to the public."

Council Member Carol Schwartz said, "DCWASA wanted to keep us in the dark, and they did."

DCWASA officials say the problems are most common in homes built during the first half of the 20th century, including those in the Capitol Hill and Adams Morgan sections.

February 13, 2004   DCWASA's Web site invites customers to three community meetings to discuss lead information. These meetings are to take place on February 18, February 26, and March 2.

In anticipation of the upcoming community meetings, DCWASA and the EPA need to be clear and consistent in communicating their message to the public.

Questions for Discussion   To consider this crisis from an ethical perspective, answer the following questions:

1.   What parties are at fault?

2.   What might DCWASA have done differently to promote a different outcome?

3.   What are the ethical consequences of the company's actions?

4.   How could the EPA's actions been different, given its role to protect the public?

5.   When is controlling information in a crisis ethical and when is it not?

6.   What types of "damage control" are unintentionally dishonest?

7.   What could reporters, public officials, and the public do based on the current crisis? Put yourself in the role of "public servant." Keeping the public's welfare in mind, how might you respond?

8.   How would you characterize Glenn Gerstell's responses?

---

[4] When I called the number in early February, I got this message from DCWASA's voice-mail box: "Sorry, you cannot leave a message now because this user's mailbox is full."

Answer the Following Questions

1. With what type of crisis are DCWASA and the EPA dealing?
2. What is the cause of the crisis? How stable is it? How controllable is it?
3. Evaluate the communication strategy to date. How effective do you think it's been with the public?
4. Given your answers to numbers 1–3 above, what next steps would you take in formulating a communication strategy from February 11 forward?

Possible Assignment

Your Role

Chairman of the Board at DCWASA.

Your Task

Given the type and cause of the crisis DCWASA experienced, choose one or more crisis communication strategies. Use that approach to write an open letter to DCWASA customers that you can insert in the next bill, post to the company's Web site, and publish in the *Washington Post*. In addition, create an opening statement of up to five minutes to the public and press that you can deliver at the February 18 community meeting.

Your Audience

The public (your customers) and the press.

References

Cohn, D. "District Residents Seek Tests for Lead; Fears of Tap Water Contamination Prompt Screenings." *Washington Post,* February 4, 2004.

Davis, Tom. "Public Confidence, Down the Drain. The Federal Role in Ensuring Safe Drinking Water in the District of Columbia." Congressional Hearing, March 5, 2004. http://reform.house.gov/GovReform/Hearings/EventSingle.aspx?EventID=797.

District of Columbia Water and Sewer Authority. (n.d.) http://www.dcwasa.com. Accessed February 2004.

Environmental Protection Agency. (n.d.) "Drinking Water Security Outreach Materials." http://www.epa.gov/safewater/security/flyers/index.html. Accessed February 23, 2004.

Holly, D. "WASA Ready to Issue Filters as Testing for Lead Contamination Continues." *The Associated Press,* March 1, 2004.

Johnson, J. N. "New Water Quality Report Now Available. Your Drinking Water Has Met or Surpassed All Federal Standards Everyday in 2001," June 21, 2002. http://www.dcwasa.com/news/listings/alert_detail51.cfm. Accessed February 23, 2004.

"Lead in Drinking Water Notice for District of Columbia Residents." (n.d.) Visited site http://www.epa.gov/region03/leaddc.htm. Accessed February 23, 2004.

Leonnig, C., and A. Goldstein. "D.C. Handling of Lead Issue Blaster on Hill." *Washington Post,* March 6, 2004.

McClintock, M. "Learning More About Lead." *Washington Post,* February 5, 2004.

McElhatton, J. "WASA Head Concedes Agency Failing." *Washington Times,* February 12, 2004.

Nakamura, D. "Water in D.C. Exceeds EPA Lead Limit." *Washington Post,* January 31, 2004.

Nakamura, D. "Davis Assails Water Agency of Lead Risk." *Washington Post,* February 3, 2004.

Nakamura, D. "Water Agency Fired Manager Who Warned of D.C. Lead." February 4, 2004.

Nakamura, D. "WASA Avoided Replacing Lead Service Lines." *Washington Post,* February 11, 2004.

Nakamura, D. "D.C. Homes Urged to Flush Taps Longer; Water Authority Revises Time it Takes to Lower the Lead Level." *Washington Post,* February 19, 2004.

Nakamura, D. "EPA Failed to Hold D.C. Accountable, Some Say." *Washington Post,* February 23, 2004.

Nakamura, D., and D. Cohn. "D.C. to Create WASA Task Force; Water Agency Accused of Not Revealing Data on High Lead Levels." *Washington Post,* February 5, 2004.

Nakamura, D., and D. Cohn. "Experts Seek Answers on Tainted D.C. Water." *Washington Post,* February 8, 2004.

Nakamura, D, and N. Tucker. "Council Faults Handling of Lead Contamination." *Washington Post,* February 1, 2004.

Nurnberger, L. "Why City Authorities Failed to Notify Washington, DC, Residents That Thousands of Homes Have Elevated Lead Levels." Transcript. National Public Radio (NPR).

Olson, E. "Why Didn't They Get the Lead Out?" *Washington Post,* February 8, 2004.

Rosenberg, J. "High Levels of Lead in Washington, DC, Drinking Water." Transcript. *Marketplace,* March 1, 2004.

Index

Note: Page numbers followed by *n* indicate material in footnotes.